the Once and Future Jesus

the Once and Future Jesus

The Jesus Seminar

Robert W. Funk

Thomas Sheehan

Marcus J. Borg

John Shelby Spong

Karen L. King

John Dominic Crossan

Lloyd Geering

Gerd Lüdemann

Walter Wink

Polebridge
Press

The Once and Future Jesus

Published in 2000 by Polebridge Press, P. O. Box 6144, Santa Rosa, California, 95406.

Library of Congress Cataloging-in-Publication Data

The once and future Jesus / The Jesus Seminar
    p. cm.
Includes bibliographical references.
ISBN 0-944344-80-1 (pbk.)
    1. Jesus Christ — Historicity, 2. Christianity — Forecasting. 3. Jesus Seminar. I. Jesus Seminar.

BT303.2 .O53 2000
232 — dc21   00-042768

contents

Gregory C. Jenks

Introduction

T his collection brings together into a single volume the various keynote addresses — all by Fellows of the Jesus Seminar — from the *Once & Future Jesus* celebration at Santa Rosa, California in October 1999.

Like the panel sessions that were interspersed through the program, those addresses were organized around three themes: The Future of Jesus, The Future of the Church, and The Future of the Faith.

The event which provided the context for these addresses was a double celebration.

It was in part a celebration of the creative and collaborative scholarship undertaken by the Fellows of the Jesus Seminar, in dialogue with a wider community of Associate members of the Westar Institute, over some fifteen years. With work on the sayings and deeds of Jesus now completed, the Seminar had come to a significant milestone in its life. That was worth celebrating.

The event was also planned with an eye to the significance of the year 2000 in the popular consciousness. The passing of approximately two thousand years since the time of Jesus has prompted considerable interest in the media and in society generally. No other figure has had such an impact on Western culture. Even cultures largely untouched by the Jesus tradition until the European expansion in the last few centuries have been drawn into the excitement of this anniversary.

Clearly, the two milestones at the center of the *Once & Future Jesus* event are of quite different orders of magnitude. No one suggests that fifteen years of collaborative scholarly research are comparable to the brief incandescence of Jesus' historic activity, nor the subsequent impact of his legacy on humanity.

Yet the juxtaposition of these two celebrations is fortuitous. Over time the Jesus tradition has been elaborated and developed in

1

diverse contexts and with multiple variants. In the process, many opposing positions have developed. These include churchman and heretic, prelate and protestant, mystic and social activist, scholar and revivalist — to name but a few.

If it is to function as a positive cultural stream within our emerging global society, the diverse Jesus tradition requires critique. This is not because historical reconstruction enjoys any priority over traditional (or even canonical) expressions of that tradition. Rather, the critique is needed because the authentic Jesus materials — to the extent that they might be recoverable — deserve to be identified and valued for their own sake. And also because those people and institutions who invoke the Jesus tradition should be publicly accountable for the ways in which their elaboration of that material is undertaken.

The Jesus Seminar has a made seminal contribution to the recovery, critique and evaluation of the earliest Jesus traditions.

The Seminar held its first meeting at Berkeley in 1985. Some 30 scholars gathered at the invitation of Robert Funk to identify an agreed inventory of sayings and actions by Jesus that could serve as a database for Jesus studies.

Since then the Seminar has met twice a year as the project grew beyond the expectations of the original participants. What was thought likely to require two or three meetings has proved to be a much more challenging — and rewarding — task. It has also attracted unparalleled media attention, and the ire of numerous critics.

Over the intervening years more than two hundred scholars have participated in the Jesus Seminar. Many of the original members continue as Fellows, while others have moved their attention to other research interests. There have typically been a little over 75 Fellows at any one time.

The work of the Jesus Seminar has been characterized by the distinctive ethos that has developed as it went about its work. Early in its life the Seminar made several decisions that were to be formative for its subsequent development.

A commitment was made always to come to a decision, rather than to be satisfied with an exchange of scholarly views. The discipline that this imposed has ensured that the Seminar retained its cutting edge as questions were pursued to the point of closure; however tentative some conclusions might need to be.

Another significant decision was that the results of the Seminar's deliberations were to be reported in non technical language for the information of those who are not specialists in religion, including the Associate members of Westar. The Seminar's related decision to vote using a four color schema fortuitously provided a simple yet effective means of expressing the range of scholarly views — as well as the consensus through a weighted average result.

Together with the collaborative ethos of the Seminar, and its independence from religious and academic institutions, these have proved to be critical choices for shaping the history and the character of the Jesus Seminar. The end result has been a sustained cooperative scholarly effort over more than fifteen years, and a distinctive camaraderie between the participants.

The research agenda of the Seminar has passed through three clear phases. In the first phase, the focus was on more than 1,500 versions of approximately 500 sayings attributed to Jesus in the first three centuries after his death. Of these, just 90 sayings were judged to have some probable authenticity, and were coded red or pink. This constitutes approximately 18% of the total inventory, including both canonical and non-canonical traditions.

In the second phase, the deeds of Jesus came under scrutiny. This included things he was said to have done, as well as actions reported to have been done to him by others. The Fellows examined 387 reports of 176 events, in most of which Jesus was the principal actor. Of these only 10 were given a red rating, with another 19 colored pink. The 29 events considered authentic represent a mere 16% of the total inventory, again including both canonical and non-canonical traditions.

The third phase of the Jesus Seminar's work has been to produce profiles of Jesus, drawing on the material identified for the common inventory. A considerable number of profiles has been prepared. They evidence significant common insights into the person and mission of Jesus, while still reflecting considerable difference in interpretation.

The results of the Seminar's work have been reported widely. In addition to publication in *The Fourth R* and *Forum*, two major reports have been appeared: *The Five Gospels. The Search for the Authentic Words of Jesus.* (Macmillan, 1993) and *The Acts of Jesus. The Search for the Authentic Deeds of Jesus.* (HarperSanFrancisco, 1998). A volume on the profiles of Jesus is in preparation.

Other significant publications include *The Complete Gospels* (Polebridge, 1994) and *The Gospel of Jesus According to the Jesus Seminar* (Polebridge, 1999).

With the wide dissemination of its findings, the Jesus Seminar has entered another phase of its work. Individual and communities across North America and around the globe have taken a profound interest in the significance of these results for themselves. Requests for Jesus Seminar on the Road programs have multiplied, along with invitations for international appearances by leading members of the Seminar.

These essays celebrate the scholarship and the results of the Jesus Seminar. More than that, they probe the character and the significance of the Jesus tradition.

Gregory C. Jenks
Associate Director
Westar Institute

Robert W. Funk

the Once and Future Jesus

The End of the Old
the Advent of the New

Turbulence and turmoil

We have come to the end of an era. The advent of a new millennium is merely an outward sign of the metamorphosis taking place. During the half century that separates us from World War II, momentous changes have taken place in our world — social, political, economic, cultural, religious, and especially mythic. It is possible here only to name them. Yet they are foundational to everything we have done and will do at sessions of the Jesus Seminar.

First of all, the mythic universe that furnished the frame of reference for our Western myths and creeds for more than two millennia is crumbling, in spite of popular reaffirmations to the contrary. The checkout stand of the local supermarket is not a reliable guide to what has happened to the mythical worldview that has supported Christian orthodoxy for the last two millennia. The world was not created six thousand years ago, along with individual species, as many once believed. The world will not end in a fiery holocaust at the hands of an angry God, as the book of Revelation suggests. And God does not dabble from time to time in the history of special peoples, as the Bible claims. These former mythic certainties are all gone.

When John Paul II announces that heaven and hell are metaphors, we know that the decay of the old cosmological myths is well advanced. After all, it took him and the Roman church nearly three and a half centuries to recognize and admit the injustice done to Galileo.

Secondly, we have come to the end of the Christian era — the end of the hegemony of the christianized, industrialized West. That hegemony has given way to a global era, in which a world-wide econ-

5

omy, a universal technology, mass consumption, and instant communication between all parts of the globe have altered perceptions forever. And that is only part of the information revolution now in progress. For better or worse, we now inhabit a multi-cultural world in which Christianity and Judaism must compete with other religious traditions as old or older than themselves. We cannot put these developments back in the tribal bag, try as many ethnic groups will. This transition has enormous consequences for the future of Jesus, the church, and the faith.

The end of the Christian era is marked further by the decline of religious literacy. Religious literacy in American society has degenerated steadily in this century until knowledge of the basic components of the Christian tradition has reached an appalling low. The churches have all but abandoned their traditional role in education. The mainline churches have by and large adopted a defensive posture: they have raised the drawbridge and manned the battlements against women and gays, and against critical knowledge of Christian origins. The enemy turns out to be their own insecurities.

Retreat in one area breeds retreat in another. Scholars of religion are exiting Christian precincts at an alarming rate in order to gain the right to think unorthodox thoughts. Biblical scholarship and theology are moving into a wholly profane, secular setting. Many scholars have elected the safe route, which is to abandon the theological ship and seek refuge in a humanistic harbor.

The departure of scholars is matched, or perhaps exceeded, by the loss of clergy. The clergy have been caught in the tension between the churches they have taken oaths to serve and the scholars who were their mentors in seminaries. Like other rational human beings, some have opted for the safe course, which is not to offend patrons of the parish in order to protect their pensions. This intellectual sacrifice has made them theological eunuchs in the temple of the Lord. Others have given up and quit the service of the church altogether. Still others — a few — have dared to broach the fundamental issues and behave like prophets, at great expense to themselves. A handful told the truth as they knew it from the start.

The mainline denominations, which are in fact oldline denominations, are in danger of becoming sideline denominations, as John Cobb warns. They have lost members at an alarming rate. Denominational loyalties have eroded. Their bureaucracies, however, remain mired down in parochialism, intransigent fiefdoms, and a medieval mentality.

To top it off, there is the sense among many liberal-minded people that we have been betrayed by the Bible. In the half century just ending, there is belated recognition that biblically based Christianity has espoused causes that no thinking or caring person is any longer willing to endorse. We have had enough of the persecution of Jews and witches; of the justification of black slavery; of the suppression of women, sex, and sexuality; and of the stubborn defense of a male-dominated, self-serving clergy. The Bible is not to be blamed for all this misplaced self-righteousness; how we have employed it is at fault. We have created a mindless authoritarian bibliolatry. For Protestants, the office of holy inquisition has been the Bible. Religious and cultural wars are again being fought across the pages of the Bible over sexuality, the place of women in society, and special creation. We cannot, we must not, shrink from engagement with the ignorance and misunderstanding that fuels such egregious misuse of scripture.

The final transition we are making is the reconciliation of religion with the sciences. Giordano Bruno was burned at the stake on 17 February 1600 for insisting, in opposition to the church, that the earth revolved around the sun. He was a champion of Copernican cosmology and Galileo's telescope. The church pretended it knew better. That pretension would have been bad enough, but the church would not tolerate dissent. Accordingly, the church rejected the sciences and prostituted history in defense of its own dogmas. It is now paying the price: Today, according to Roger Jones, "it is science that dictates to the church and not vice versa. . . . It is science and not religion that gives today's world its rationale, morality, sustenance, and story of creation, such as it is." (*Physics for the Rest of Us,* 1992) At the very least, theology must be rejoined to the sciences. We cannot afford another extended divorce.

Meanwhile, we can do something about the rape of history for apologetic purposes conducted by Bible scholars and theologians as well-meaning friends of the churches. The end of the violation of history is what the renewed quest is all about. We have, I trust, advanced the cause of respect for the integrity of the past as the basic ethic guiding our work.

Renewal of the quest

The renewal of the quest of the historical Jesus in the 1970s signaled the desire to return to origins, to the beginning, to learn again what it meant and means to be a follower of Jesus of Nazareth. This quest was not born of idle curiosity, pursued by academics who had nothing better to do; it is a quest for the holy grail, for the innocence of a meal taken with toll collectors and sinners, when the Jesus movement was young, amorphous, and in a life and death struggle to find its way in the world. The renewed quest is the herald of a radical reformation — the recovery of the once and the projection of the future Jesus.

These are high sounding words, to be sure. Yet consider what the eight platform lecturers have contributed to the renewal of the quest and the search for a credible faith.

Tom Sheehan anticipated the Seminar in 1986 with his book, *The First Coming. How the Kingdom of God Became Christianity.* In that book, Tom wrote "Jesus had freed himself from religion and apocalypse by transforming hope into charity and by recasting future eschatology as present liberation." (191) The clarity of Tom's picture gave heart to the rest of us who were only beginning to find our way. Tom was the harbinger of the quest even then aborning.

Marc Borg launched his own quest in 1984 with *Conflict, Holiness and Politics in the Teaching of Jesus.* He followed in 1987 with *Jesus: A New Vision* and then with *Meeting Jesus Again for the First Time* (1994). The Jesus one meets in these pages has been imbibed by thousands who act as though they were dying of thirst on a spiritual desert. In *Meeting Jesus Again,* Marc wrote that the notion that God's only son came to this planet to offer his life as a sacrifice for the sins of the world is simply incredible. (131) The interpretation of Jesus as both high priest and final sacrificial victim was meant to displace the religion of the second temple, but instead it became the vehicle for retaining and maintaining temple religion under new auspices.

Dominic Crossan joined the parables parade early on its modern history. His little book, *Dark Interval,* published originally in 1975, sketches a theory of parable that underlies his *In Parables* (1973). He pioneered the study of Jesus' aphorisms in *In Fragments* (1983). His ground-breaking study of the passion narrative, *Who Killed Jesus? (1995),* challenged Christian anti-Semitism at its narrative roots. And of course his revolutionary biographies of Jesus have mesmerized hordes of readers. I hear people speaking glibly about "open commensality" and "radical egalitarianism" as though they were phrases heard on the evening news.

The irony of the German theological tradition is that Gerd Lüdemann is battling for his academic life when he should be honored as a legitimate successor to D. F. Strauss. He has written books on the resurrection, on the virgin birth, on the heretics in early Christianity, and on the unholy in scripture, along with important studies of Paul. He has finally been driven to renounce Christianity as a result of what he regards as the great deception on the part of both conservative and liberal theologians. His spiritual home, he says, is the Jesus Seminar. His evangelical colleagues want him out of the theological faculty because, they insist, the scientific study of religion does not and cannot conflict with the dogmas of the Lutheran church. The great German critical tradition seems to have died in the Göttingen faculty in spite of Gerd's efforts to keep it alive.

Karen King has become the principal advocate of what she calls "the radical historicization of Christianity." By that she means the recovery of the *stories* of Christian origins conceived and written apart from the norms and boundaries of canonical and orthodox views. To that end she has insisted on exposing traces of women's roles in the early movement and of the nature and function of various forms of gnosticism now that the Nag Hammadi library is available to us. She wonders what is left to us now that the transcendent essence of Christianity has evaporated? Her answer: we have the history of Christianity itself. Its whole history. Those stories are rarely told in the lust for theological norms. "The variety of early Christianities, the diversity of Christianity globally, and the polyvalence of appropriation make it programmatic" for her that "Christianity does not have a single, monolithic meaning." The loss of this sense of the whole owes, in part, to the separation of history and theology into separate disciplines, and the domination of the categories of historical study by theological norms.

Walter Wink has perhaps done more than any other Fellow of the Seminar to translate the message of Jesus into a powerful new idiom for the modern world. He has marched through Chile and South Africa and the streets of New York identifying and then unmasking the powers and exposing the domination system they represent. The system, he writes in his new book, *The Powers That Be. Theology for a New Millennium,* "is characterized by unjust economic relations, oppressive political relations, biased race relations, and the use of violence to maintain them all." (p. 39) But Jesus opposed the system with every fiber of his being in the tangible crossroads of life, and he spelled out his opposition in fragments of his vision. In the tradition of Martin Luther King, Jr. and Mahatma Gandhi, Walter has taken on many a Goliath with a few soft words and an iron will to resist non-violently. He concludes his profile of Jesus with this Voltaire-inspired statement: "If Jesus had never lived, we would not have been able to invent him." (p. 81)

Lloyd Geering has brought an entire nation around to a new way of viewing the Christian faith, and he began his campaign when the rest of us were still safely ensconced in neo-orthodoxy. Back in the 1965, he wrote an essay on the resurrection for which he was eventually awarded a trial for heresy. Although he escaped the ultimate condemnation, he proceeded to take on the whole of New Zealand and much of Australia in his theological work. He did not begin his quest with the historical Jesus, but with a quest for a credible faith. In his recent book, *Tomorrow's God* (1994), he suggests that we began this century with the conviction that God created human beings in the divine image, but now at the threshold of a new century we have come to understand that human beings created God pretty much in their own image. *The World to Come: From Christian Past to Global Future*, just off the press, suggests that we have come not just to the end of the millennium, but to the end of Christendom, the dissolution of Christian orthodoxy, the failure of modernism, and the end of mythic certainty. As we enter the new millennium, we must find a new global spirituality that preserves the best from our collective pasts and promotes care for all living creatures and the earth itself. Lloyd became an honorary Fellow of the Jesus Seminar in 1998.

Bishop John Shelby Spong is also an honorary Fellow of the Seminar. Bishop Spong has rescued the Bible from fundamentalism, exposed the resurrection as a misunderstanding, denied that the virgin birth can be understood literally, and insisted that the church must change or die. He has been the ecclesiastical champion of women and gays. And that is only the beginning. His twelve theses form the basis of a new reformation; they invite review and debate as we enter the third millennium. While the quest has not been at the base of his program, his vision of Jesus the historical figure has. Jack Spong towers above ecclesiastical officials in the world today like the colossus of Rhodes. He is the colossus of Morristown. Bishop Spong and Lloyd Geering bring a dimension to the Jesus Seminar that moves our work beyond the minutiae of academic exegesis into the ecclesiastical trenches.

Summary. It is the vision that Jesus had of God's domain, not the myth of God incarnate, that is the bedrock of our discovery. The rediscovery of this vision was provoked initially by the collapse of the old mythical framework: the disintegration of the myth sent us in search of something beyond and behind the myth. Even if our reconstruction of the historical figure turns out to be incorrect, or only partially accurate, the Jesus of the creeds, the myth of the external redeemer, will go on crumbling because it no longer coheres with the worldview that is its living frame of reference — the new myth of origins and destiny provided us by Copernicus, Newton, Darwin, Einstein, and quantum physics.

The Jesus Seminar

Protocol. The first steps we took in organizing the Jesus Seminar back in 1985 turned out to be crucial. We agreed from the outset to form an agenda of issues on which we would *come to decision*, no matter how provisional or tentative. That in itself is uncharacteristic of humanists who prefer to hold all questions open pending further review. We adopted *collaboration* as our group process in order to expand the basis of decision-making. We agreed to make our work *cumulative*, which meant that we focused on what we had in common rather than concentrate on our differences. Academic critics of scholarly essays tend to make the worst case they can for the publications of their colleagues, whereas the friendly critics of great literary works attempt to make the best case they can for their authors. We have behaved against type in striving to make the *best case for our texts and each other*, without blunting our critical acumen. This, I judge, has been our sharpest departure from academic protocol that has resulted in our most significant achievement: the production of knowledge that makes a difference.

It may have been fortuitous that we assembled *outside the university* (although we started briefly inside). We gathered beyond the earshot of the churches, even beyond the reach of the seminaries. By dint of historical circumstance, we formed the Seminar outside the boundaries of the professional guilds. That made it possible for us to establish different protocols. We did all of this at some risk to ourselves.

We insisted on holding our *sessions in public* and making *reports* in non-technical language that any literate person could understand. Voting with colored beads and reporting with color-coded texts were ingredient to those aims. We took some additional risk in talking to reporters and appearing on talk shows. This aspect of our work has generated the most controversy. Our critics evidently think it preferable to keep learning elitist by keeping it to themselves.

We recognized at the outset that we are all facing an information glut in the electronic age. We are being bombarded with unsorted and undigested information from every quarter. On the subject of religion, the common view is that one opinion is as good as another. This conviction is a recipe for chaos, and that is just about what we have. By banding together and keeping our eye on a common goal, we had hoped to reduce confusion by a small fraction in *The Five Gospels* and *The Acts of Jesus*. It is too early to say whether we have succeeded.

The inexplicable consensus

The Fellows of the Jesus Seminar believe we have isolated some traces of the historical figure of Jesus. These traces can be described as finger prints left on characteristic deeds and a voice print based on distinctive patterns and content of speech. Some Fellows frame these clues in larger sociological or anthropological models utilizing cross cultural data. The profiles of Jesus that have emerged from our common database bear remarkable resemblances to each other. The similarities in our individual portraits of Jesus look like collusion to our critics. How do we explain the consensus that has formed around the evidence and its interpretation?

I can best explain this striking harmonic convergence by comparing and contrasting the protocols of the Seminar with those of our vocal critics.

Vocal critics. In the first place, the Fellows of the Seminar discerned early on in their work that a paradigm shift was taking place. The old view advocated by Johannes Weiss and made popular by Albert Schweitzer that Jesus was an apocalyptic or endtime prophet was crumbling. Marcus Borg, who had just returned from England and was therefore innocent of the parables movement, sensed that shift and polled the Seminar and the profession to demonstrate that it was in fact so. The position of the Seminar immediately became *distinctive* in recognizing that a shift was taking place. The distinctive position of the Seminar had as its corollary Jesus as a *distinctive* Galilean sage. The paradigm shift and the emergence of a new profile of Jesus reinforced each other.

Our critics, meanwhile, continued to insist that Jesus was an average Jew, who, according to them, believed and advocated what every average Jew believed and advocated — that the end of the age was at hand. If he did not share that view, and if he did not express that view in Aramaic, then we had robbed him of his Jewishness. Few of our critics have recognized what a denigrating view of Second Temple Judaism that is.

By looking for a single voice in a Galilean crowd the Seminar launched its quest as a discovery venture. Our critics responded by turning their so-called third quest into an apology for the orthodox view.

In the Seminar we took as our primary problem how the Jesus tradition got from around 30 C.E. to the first narrative gospel, Mark, in the 70s. Our critics adopt the synoptic gospels as their starting point and roam around in those gospels indiscriminately as though the authors were eyewitnesses of the original events. They see no need to reckon with the forms of anecdotes that served as vehicles for the memories of Jesus, and they take no notice of the formal structure of sayings that were likely to have survived twenty to fifty years or more of oral transmission. With the exception of the extremely conservative scholars, most do agree, however, that the Gospel of John is virtually worthless as a source of information about Jesus.

It is worth taking note of the steady canonical bias in the protests of our critics. They use the synoptics as though they were virtually reliable history, but reject all extra-canonical sources as secondary and worthless. They deride our use of Q and Thomas and the other fragmentary gospels.

In spite of the fact that the parables appear in their canonical sources, our critics refuse to make use of them as distinctive traces of Jesus' voice, because, they argue, who can say what the parables mean? The aphorisms, too, come in for short shrift because they blend in with the wisdom tradition of Israel! These deft moves permit them to ignore the primary database we have identified, using both form and content as clues, as essential to the rediscovery of the historical figure.

The alternative view our critics propose is to begin with the deeds of Jesus. Yet they have trouble isolating any particular deed as the bedrock of the tradition, beyond Jesus' baptism at the hands of John and the crucifixion — events no one contests who thinks Jesus was a historical person. They do not recognize the fundamental methodological problem put so pointedly by Julian Hills: the deeds of Jesus are *reported*, while the sayings of Jesus are *repeated*. In other words, deeds are narrated from a third person perspective, while the authentic words of Jesus betray his own perspective. In any case, the deeds of Jesus are only literary artifacts apart from some interpretive assessment, and it only Jesus who can really tell us what his acts were all about. For this his sayings are essential.

In clinging to the apocalyptic hypothesis, our critics are disposed to be literal-minded: the apocalyptic tradition is relentlessly literal and humorless. It is difficult to crack a joke if you think the world is about to end. And, of course, having a celebration just before Armageddon seems inappropriate. The Seminar, on the other hand, by paying close attention to the parables and witticisms of Jesus find them filled with metaphor, hyperbole, parody, paradox, and ambiguity. The contrast between Jesus' authentic words and the apocalyptic tradition could not be stronger.

It is striking that none of our critics, so far as I can see, ever refers to the collapse of the mythic universe or the information revolution through which we are passing. They seem to think the old symbols are still in place and functional. But then I can see why they do so: The credibility of the apocalyptic worldview requires it.

Pursuing the puzzle. One of my teachers taught me to beware of the scholar who can account for all the data. You can be sure he or she is manipulating the evidence. Let your research begin with what your predecessors have left unexplained. It was profound advice. Start with the puzzle others have not been able to solve. The puzzle we began with was why the parables and aphorisms, and the metaphorical language of Jesus, which play such a large role in the gospels, found so little place in the earlier quests.

In pursuing this puzzle, we adopted the broad scholarly consensus on the history and relationships of the gospels. We affirmed with most scholars that Matthew and Luke were essentially revisions of Mark. We did not permit ourselves to make use of their revisions of Mark without powerful corroborating evidence. We assumed that Matthew and Luke also made use of the Sayings Gospel Q in supplementing Mark. We struggled with the difficulties in reconstructing the original text of Q. We acknowledged that some stray oral traditions may have been captured by Matthew and Luke. And we even conceded that the Fourth Gospel may have preserved some incidental historical data. For example, we took seriously the observation that the first followers of Jesus were probably recruited from disciples of John in the Jordan Valley. We agreed that the Gospel of Thomas was useful in reconstructing the history of some individual traditions, as were other fragments of gospels. But nothing in our profiles of Jesus depends solely on data taken from Thomas or other extra-canonical source.

In our deliberations we held ourselves to the strict observance of this consensus. We did not permit each other to fudge. Out of dozens of individual decisions about particular sayings and parables, in retrospect we formulated rules of evidence. Those rules reflect actual practice rather the theory of how the tradition grew and developed. It was on the basis of this complex method that we arrived at a shared database, which in turn produced profiles with remarkable affinities. Those profiles are not monolithic, to be sure. But they do converge at many points. Our critics are flabbergasted at the economy of the results. They cannot believe that two academics, much less seventy-five or more, could exercise that much discipline over fifteen years of close collaboration. On some days I have trouble believing it myself.

Fragments of a Vision

A glimpse of a glimpse

The voice of Jesus emanates from the compendium of parables, aphorisms, and dialogues we have isolated from the mass of the Jesus tradition. In those sayings, and correlative acts, we can occasionally catch sight of Jesus' vision of God's domain. Visions come in bits and pieces, to be sure, in random stunning insights; they never come in self-enclosed systems. Yet from the fragments of insight one can begin to piece together some sense of the whole. That is what we have done in producing profiles of Jesus. A profile is nothing more than drawing lines connecting dozens of the provocative insights we have detected in the words and deeds of Jesus. As a result of these small successes, we occasionally catch a glimpse of his glimpse of that domain he called God's.

I propose now to compile a short list of seven insights as I perceive them, and then, subsequently, translate them into terms that apply to the Jesus Seminar and the Westar Institute.

Jesus as sage

Jesus' characteristic speech forms, and the content of his language, indicate that he belongs to the wisdom tradition of Israel — along with Job, Proverbs, Ecclesiastes, the Wisdom of ben Sirach, and the Wisdom of Solomon. In the New Testament, the Letter of James is a wisdom tract. Wisdom is not concerned with theories of sin and salvation, but with how to cope with life. We have identified Jesus as a sage rather than as a lawgiver or a prophet.

Jesus as exorcist

We agreed in the Seminar that Jesus was an exorcist by a huge margin. We hedged that conclusion by expressing our collective doubt about the existence of demons in the ancient sense. I will speak later of the kinds of demons with which we have to deal in our world.

Trust is the horizon of the kingdom

Most of us in Western industrialized societies are immersed in a work ethic: we labor to produce the goods of life and the good life and believe our virtue resides in that labor. On the other hand, Jesus advocated a trust ethic.

He admonished his followers to take no thought for the morrow, for food, for clothing, for shelter. The flowers of the field and the birds of the sky were his paradigms of trust (Luke 12:22–25, 27–28).

Like the Israelites wandering in the Sinai desert, disciples are never to ask for more than one day's bread at a time (Matt 6:11). They need not plan ahead, for (Luke 11:9–10):

> Ask — it'll be given you;
> seek — you'll find;
> knock — it'll be opened for you.

Kinship in the kingdom

Somewhere near the heart of Jesus' vision is this simple admonition that has inspired and troubled Jesus' followers from the very first: "love your enemies" (Luke 6:27b//Matt 5:44b).

Love your enemies is an action statement: it recommends that we do something, presumably some activity appropriate to God's domain. If we take the rhetorical complex in which this saying is embedded as a faithful exposition of the sense of the admonition, then we would have to say that loving one's enemies imitates the divine disposition. A little later in the Q sequence, we are told, if you do this, "you'll be children of the Most High" (Luke 6:35b//Matt 5:45a). God, it seems,

> causes the sun to rise on both the bad and the good,
> and sends rain on both the just and the unjust (Matt 5:45b).

That's the basis of a fairly radical notion of God. A God who treats all human beings evenhandedly is not in much evidence in either testament. The God pictured there is highly partial and often quite vindictive.

In a world emerging from tribal cultures, Jesus' saying struck his hearers as truly radical. In formulating it, Jesus is marking the transition from the ethnic phase of human societies to the transethnic phase, as Lloyd Geering puts it. Of course, we have not made much progress towards that new phase in the last two millennia, but even now we are entering the global phase of human development, which makes Jesus' admonition even more pertinent.

Love your enemies is probably the most radical thing Jesus ever said. Unless, of course, one considers the parable of the Samaritan. There the admonition is to let your enemies love you.

The next most radical aphorism is perhaps the harshest of all the sayings in the Jesus repertoire. "Unless you hate your father and mother, and wife and children and brothers and sisters — yes, even life itself — you're no disciple of mine" (Luke 14:26).

This saying is about breaking the ties that bind. Christians have been inclined to ignore this saying for most of its history, or have remodeled it. Matthew has simply turned the saying around to make it more acceptable to polite society: "If you love your father and mother more than me. . . . you are not worthy of me" (Matt 10:37). His community did not like, or did not understand, the radical demand in its original form.

Jesus was probably thinking of an extended family, perhaps of three or four or five generations, living in a one or two room house, presided over by an aging patriarch who made life and death decisions for everyone in the family. Under such circumstances, he might well have indicated that his followers must break their ties with the family enclave in order to be open to the radically new way of relating to God's domain. That makes eminent sense. Especially if we do not insist that he meant "hate" literally.

The contrast between the love of enemies and the hatred of family is striking. The one blows away the tribal boundary, the other demolishes family ties. Kinship in the kingdom means dwelling in a house without walls.

Celebrating the fiction of the kingdom

Celebration is the by-product of trust. It is also the joy attendant upon not being left out.

One reason many of us in the Seminar believe Jesus could not have been an apocalyptic prophet who expected the world to end momentarily is his impulse to celebrate. Apocalyptic is for those who mourn the corruption of creation, who think they have been cheated in the game of life; it is not a program for the future; it is the counsel of endtime despair.

Celebration runs like a golden thread through the authentic stories and witticisms of Jesus. In the parable of the Dinner Party, the nobodies in the street become privileged guests, hinting at a symposium, an evening of conviviality. Dinner for three is transformed into a banquet for dozens (Luke 14:16–24//Thom 64:1–12//Matt 22:1–14).

The disciples of John the Baptist fast and so do the Pharisees, but Jesus and his disciples do not fast. To this observation Jesus responds, "The groom's friends can't fast while the groom is present, can they?" (Mark 2:19). A wedding and fasting are simply incompatible. The styles of Jesus and John are contrasted in a passage Luke and Matthew have taken from Q:

> John the Baptist appeared on the scene, eating no bread and drinking no wine, and you say, "He is demented," This mother's son appeared on the scene both eating and drinking, and you say, "There is a glutton and a drunk, a crony of toll collectors and sinners (Luke 7:31–35//Matt 11:16–19).

The Baptist is said to have a demon because he was a strict ascetic. Jesus, on the other hand, apparently dined frequently with toll collectors and sinners (Mark 2:16). In addition, he told many stories in which celebration was a theme.

A woman loses a coin, sweeps the dirt floor of her house to find it, and then spends her new found coin to celebrate her good fortune (Luke 15:8–9).

A shepherd goes in search of a wayward sheep, and when he finds it he calls for a celebration, which usually required the slaughter of a lamb (Luke 15:4–5).

In sum, Jesus was a celebrant of life with all its ups and downs, ins and outs, successes and disappointments. He was a celebrant of the fiction of the kingdom. *L'chaim!*

Humor, humility & morality

Jesus' parables and aphorisms are laced with humor in the form of parody, paradox, hyperbole, and ambiguity. There is one further instance often overlooked. I believe the Markan version of the saying about what goes in is the original form (Mark 7:14–15):

> It's not what goes into a person that can defile;
> It's what comes out that defiles.

Jesus does not specify which orifice in the human body he had in mind when he said that. In a society without plumbing, it was what comes out of the lower orifices that commonly defiled.

In the course of transmission, however, "mouth" was added to both parts of the saying. Then, in the explanation offered to the disciples privately, there is a whole list of moralisms — thefts, murders, adulteries — only a few of which have to do with what comes out of the mouth. We can be confident that the list does not go back to Jesus. As a rule, the style of Jesus is to prefer ambiguity to flat, unequivocal admonitions.

Humor in most of its forms is inimical to moralism. Moralisms are the enemy of humor. Morality may be defined as conformity to established, sanctioned codes of behavior, of the acceptance of conventional notions of right and wrong. We have observed that Jesus was a social deviant. He was not a conformist; he was an iconoclast. He was therefore not a moralist.

The cross as the symbol of integrity

The cross is the symbol of integrity. Jesus died on the cross because he was unwilling to compromise his vision. Just as Socrates drank the hemlock rather than flee at the behest of his friends, Jesus went to the cross mute, without the support of friends. Jesus was the victim of his own vision.

The Future of Jesus

Catching sight of the vision of Jesus has been an arduous and demanding task. Up to this point it has required narrowly focused concentration on ancient records. But now it is time to begin thinking about translation. I propose to translate the seven facets of Jesus' vision into terms that apply to the Jesus Seminar and the Westar Institute.

Wisdom as literacy

The Fellows of the Jesus Seminar are engaged in the gathering and dissemination of information. We are researchers and teachers by training and instinct. We are supposed to be literate, which means possessed of learning. We have devoted our lives to making others literate. Literacy is defined as the ability to read a short paragraph and answer questions about it. In our case, we teach students to read a short paragraph in the Bible and answer reasonably sophisticated questions about that paragraph. Literacy, it seems to me, is the basic function of the Jesus Seminar and the Westar Institute. There is no nobler calling.

Jesus made people literate in a slightly different sense. He helped them to see the world in a radically new way. We may not aspire to so much, but we can still think of literacy and learning as extensions of the role of Jesus as sage.

Trust is the horizon of Jesus' vision of God's domain

Trust is the horizon of Jesus' vision of God's domain, and trust should be the compass of our entry into the next millennium.

The first step into that future is to hold a wake for the mythic certainties we have lost. Bid them farewell with thanks for two millennia of faithful service. Offer thanks to our predecessors who formulated the creeds and then struggled to interpret those formulations. Then step across the threshold of the millennium into a new future. Celebrate the opportunity to rediscover the roots of the tradition. Grab destiny by the forelock and hang on for dear life.

In the second place, trust induces us to follow the truth wherever it leads. Yet the prospect of entering a private cul-de-sac compels us to test our discoveries by sharing them with each other and with our critics. Moreover, trust also allows us to act on our best insights, provisional though they may be. We can do no better; we should do no less.

Honesty is the complement of trust

The complement of trust is integrity. The one leads inevitably to the other. We cannot trust and dissemble simultaneously. We owe it to ourselves and to our friends to be up front about where we are and how we got there.

In the opening chapter of *The Quest of the historical Jesus*, Schweitzer wrote: "The critical study of the life of Jesus has been for theology a school of honesty." (p. 5) He cites example after example of nineteenth century scholars who found the quest a cruel test of honesty. I could not help think of the members of the Seminar who struggled with issue after issue. Contrary to some of the mindless criticism we have received, we have not and do not simply see our own reflections in the bottom of a deep well. On the contrary, we have all learned the agony of coming clean. The rediscovery of the historical Jesus has modified our perceptions of ourselves, along with our perceptions of Jesus.

I suggest we inscribe a cross on the floor just behind the lectern and stand on it during our On-the-Road programs as a reminder of our commitment to the truth.

Exorcisms & the crisis of faith

We have discovered, in our Seminar-on-the-Road programs and in the classrooms where we lecture, that biblical literacy often creates a crisis of faith.

Our responsibility in the face of such crises is twofold: (1) Our first job is to create therapies to assist the transition from traditional modes of faith to new perspectives. (2) The second responsibility is to respond to questions of meaning.

Therapies. The therapies we might devise have to be related to the demons to be exorcised. Here are the common demons that take possession of us:

Bible anxieties. We need to help free our friends from the tyranny of a paper pope. We can do that by introducing them to the modern scholarship of the Bible a bit at a time. We can do that by producing new translations of ancient texts and by creating new versions of the scriptures, both first and second testaments. We can do that by discriminating biblical texts that articulate the wisdom of the prophets and sages from those that reflect ancient, culturally-conditioned perspectives. Rightly dividing the word of truth is wonderful therapy.

God anxieties. Like children, most of us want to know who is in charge of the universe. We want someone to establish the rules of belief and behavior. That is what opens the door to tyrants and God. We like to think of God as *in loco parentis* — a surrogate parent. But God steadily refuses to interfere in human affairs.

Minimally, God is the potential the future lays on the present. God stands for both the order and the chaos present in the universe. We need to feel at home in that universe without parental assurances that we can have the order without the chaos. In other words, we need to take the responsibility for ourselves, our home, and our planet.

Christ anxieties: Most of us also long for an external redeemer, one who comes from another world and does for us what we are unable or unwilling to do for ourselves. We want a superman, or a wonder woman, or a King Arthur, or a John Wayne, or the hero with a thousand faces. But that messiah hasn't come and won't come. While we wait, rehearsing apocalyptic scenarios, the crisis deepens.

The messiah we need is some random act of kindness, some bold proposal to close the hole in the ozone, some discrete move to introduce candor into politics, some new intensive care for the planet. Perhaps the messiah will come when we have broken bread with our enemies.

The justification for acting on what we have learned lies in this conviction: There is a beyond to our present knowledge. There are two senses in which this is true: first, we will inevitably learn more that will change our present perspectives; second, there is a beyond to everything we can possibly know — a horizon that continues to recede as we pursue it, like the edge of a curved universe. To wait, to hesitate, to refuse to act is the betrayal of the fundamental trust inspired by Jesus of Nazareth.

Humor: questions of meaning

The second consequence of our On-the-Road programs has been the necessity to respond to questions of meaning.

We believe we have acquired new or modified knowledge of a figure of the past. That knowledge is not itself a thing of the past, but a property of the present. Our present knowledge impinges immediately on the knowledge we previously had of Jesus of Nazareth, who, although a figure of the past, has also been appropriated culturally as a property of the present. We have not hesitated, as members of this Seminar, to permit our modified knowledge of the Jesus of the past to impact his public cultural image in the present. In so doing, we bring the results of our work as historians to bear on misinformation or mis-interpretation of a cultural icon. Put succinctly, one form of knowledge encroaches willy-nilly on the other. We cannot and should not hold these two forms of knowledge in isolation, as if we could.

We have thus far majored in the difference between fact and fiction. We can linger in the past by asking which fictions created in the first three centuries best represent, are true to, the historical figure of Jesus. In other words, we can compare and contrast fictions allegedly based on the historical figure. That is a legitimate historical enterprise.

The loss of the old mythical framework for the story of the descending/ascending redeemer, however, has provoked us to take an additional step: We have focused on the vision of Jesus rather than on the visionary, on the message rather than the messenger, because the mythic messiah has ceased to be a credible icon. Jesus has become a more realistic, engaging figure when reclothed in the tattered garments of an itinerant Galilean sage and freed from the panoply of adoration. In that guise he seems to speak more directly and powerfully to a complex world in need of simpler yet profound truths. Nevertheless, his vision has very limited use if not properly understood and translated into strong contemporary idiom. Translation understandably brings with it new and anxiety-laden demands that may well lie beyond our immediate competencies. We will have to enlist help from many quarters to succeed; and others will have to enlist our help if they hope to remain connected to the historical figure.

We can reduce the anxiety attendant upon translation if we remain in the registers Jesus himself employed: metaphorical language, polyvalent responses, overstated and understated admonitions, hyperbole, parody, paradox. Humor prevents us from becoming doctrinaire; ambiguity inhibits dogmatism. Moreover, humor and humility are twins. Humor is the antidote for arrogance and hubris. Above all, we will avoid moralistic pronouncements if we speak with tongue in cheek.

Kinship in the kingdom

Bond among Fellows. An extraordinary bond has formed among Fellows along the way. That owes, I imagine, to the fact that we have passed through innumerable crises of thought and debate, as we worked our way through one fundamental issue after another. At the moment a fresh insight or a bold assertion shattered the barrier of our previous convictions, at the moment we were thinking new thoughts, venturing into uncharted territory, the convergence of compelling convictions revealed that we were blood relatives in the quest. The history of this Seminar is the story of sharing one innovative insight after another, until it became undeniably clear that a paradigm shift in Jesus studies had taken place. And that gave us the courage to follow the trail to the end.

Bond with Associates. It has been no less fundamental in our emerging corporate life to share our findings with Associates. Coming out of the closet meant casting our ideas on an ocean of opinion to see whether they would float. Commerce with Associates became, not a corollary of our work, but a key ingredient. We had to know if the emerging picture of Jesus made sense to others outside the academic circle. The decision to share brought with it another conviction I had not really anticipated.

My experience in the On-the-Road programs has led me to conclude that scholarly debate will not determine which reconstructed picture of Jesus is more accurate. The resolution of the argument regarding the historical Jesus will not take place finally in learned books but in the public market place of real needs and viable ideas. The stridency of the response we have elicited suggests that we may have stumbled on to some real issues, issues worth defining and pursuing.

The future of the debate lies, not in the hands of academics, but in your hands, those of you who care about the Jesus tradition. You will determine which Jesus will supply the energy for this tradition in the next millennium. It is a heavy responsibility. Our responsibility as Fellows is to articulate the vision of Jesus to the best of our ability and then begin the arduous task of translating that vision into new terms for the next millennium. The end product will be the creation of many minds and lives, if, in fact, we succeed at all.

Many I meet on the road find themselves aliens in the land, exiles in or from the churches, battered by the post-modern spirit which is deeply skeptical and cynical, unimpressed with political correctness, ashamed of a political process mired in a moral morass. We suffer from the anxieties that accompany the loss of our mythical heritage. We feel insolated and helpless in a sea of confusion.

Nevertheless, we see a glimmer of hope. We refuse to surrender to despair. We are looking for a new star in the East or perhaps in the southern sky.

What binds us together is our common story. I hear it wherever I go. Betrayed by the Bible, disappointed in the churches, sometimes stonewalled by pastors and priests, but certain there is a way forward. Willing to cross party lines, eager to listen, persistent in the quest for truth. What binds us together is care for the truth, for each other, and for the earth that is our home. The symbol of this new extended family is the open table. Seated around that table, breaking bread together, one may occasionally catch sight of God's domain, somewhere just beyond the horizon.

Works Cited

Borg, Marcus J, *Conflict, Holiness and Politics in the Teaching of Jesus.* Studies in the Bible and Early Christianity, vol. 5. New York/Toronto: Edwin Mellen Press, 1984.

____, *Jesus: A New Vision: Spirit, Culture, and the Life of Discipleship.* San Francisco: Harper & Row, 1987.

____, *Meeting Jesus Again for the First Time: The Historical Jesus and the Heart of Contemporary Faith.* San Francisco: HarperSanFrancisco, 1994.

Crossan, John Dominic, *Dark Interval: Towards a Theology of Story.* Sonoma, CA: Polebridge Press, 1988.

____, *In Fragments: The Aphorisms of Jesus.* San Francisco: Harper & Row, 1983.

____, *In Parables: The Challenge of the Historical Jesus.* Sonoma, CA: Polebridge Press, 1992.

____, *Who Killed Jesus: Exposing the Roots of Anti-Semitism in the Gospel Story of the Death of Jesus.* San Francisco: HarperSanFrancisco, 1995.

Funk, Robert W. and the Jesus Seminar, *The Acts of Jesus: The Search for the Authentic Deeds of Jesus.* San Francisco: HarperSanFrancisco, 1998.

Funk, Robert W., Roy W. Hoover and the Jesus Seminar, *The Five Gospels: The Search for the Authentic Words of Jesus.* New York: Macmillan, 1993.

Geering, Lloyd, *Tomorrow's God: How We Create Our Worlds.* Wellington, NZ: Bridget Williams Books, 1994 (reprint forthcoming from Polebridge Press in 2000).

____, *The World to Come: From Christian Past to Global Future.* Santa Rosa, CA: Polebridge Press, 1999.

Jones, Roger, *Physics for the Rest of Us: Ten Basic Ideas of Twentieth-century Physics That Everyone Should Know . . . and How They have Shaped Our Culture and Consciousness.* Chicago: Contemporary Books, 1992.

Sheehan, Thomas, *The First Coming: How the Kingdom of God Became Christianity.* New York: Random House, 1986.

Schweitzer, Albert, *The Quest of the Historical Jesus: A Critical Study of Its Progress from Reimarus to Wrede.* New York: Macmillan, 1961. (Originally published in German in 1906.)

Wink, Walter, *The Powers That Be: Theology for a New Millennium.* New York: Galilee, 1998.

Thomas Sheehan

from Divinity to Infinity

A t the turn of the millennium we ask what Jesus might signify in the future that opens before us. By "Jesus" I mean his message: the reign of God that this itinerant prophet-sage preached in his parables and aphorisms, enacted in his wonders and signs, and celebrated in his manner of life.

Some, of course, would go further and claim that Jesus was the very content of what he preached, the ontological embodiment of his message, or as Origen put it centuries ago, the kingdom-of-God-in-person, *ho autobasileia*.[1] This affirmation in fact lies at the heart of the Christian tradition, and if the guardians of that orthodoxy were to answer the question we are posing today, they would say: What the Christ of faith *will* be is the same as what the Jesus of history *was*: the incarnate presence of the self-communicating God.

But this is the Jesus Seminar. Over the years the members of the Seminar have bracketed, methodologically, the legitimate claims of the Christian faith that many of its members hold, in order first to establish the most accurate historical information possible about Jesus' words and deeds, and second, though more recently, to investigate the possibilities of a religious (or for that matter non-religious) appropriation of those historical words and deeds in our own days. Using Heidegger's terms we might describe the second task as a "retrieval" of the still living possibilities latent in the prophet's message of the kingdom of God.

This hermeneutical task, with focus on both past history and present meaning, parallels the program that David Friedrich Strauss, that pioneering giant in Jesus-research, laid out in his classic work, *Das Leben Jesu* (1835–1836).[2] Strauss was quite young — barely twenty-seven years old, having just begun lecturing at Tübingen University — when this ground-breaking work vaulted him overnight into fame and no doubt into more notoriety than he wanted (he was fired forthwith from his university position and never allowed to teach again). Strauss' book was an attempt to confront the dramatic crisis that Jesus-research

27

was going through in the early nineteenth century, and it would be help-ful to review his program to see if it sheds light on the even deeper cri-sis that we are living through at the beginning of the twenty-first century: the pathos of a world of religious certitude that is fast slipping away and being replaced by a world that knows no such certitude at all.

Strauss laid out a twofold program that is still viable today, but if we follow it as radically as I argue we should, much of what Christianity is about will be lost. Today we are in a worse case than Strauss was in 1835. He kept assuring his readers that they need not fear his critique of the New Testament, that they would get their Christianity back unharmed at the other end.

> The author realizes that the inner core of Christian faith is com-pletely independent of his critical investigations. Christ's super-natural birth, his miracles, his resurrection and ascension, remain eternal truths no matter how much their reality as his-torical facts may be called into doubt.... A treatise at the end of the book will show that the dogmatic significance of the life of Jesus remains intact.[3]

Today, however, we can make no such promises. If we perform the rad-ical surgery that is required, not only will certain traditional formula-tions of faith fall by the wayside but also much of the presumed content of Christianity, and rightly so. Our only consolation is that, if we do not intervene radically and soon, the patient will die. The question right from the beginning, therefore, is how seriously, thoroughly, and deci-sively one wants to act. Strauss hardly went far enough. He claimed that the problem with traditional Christology lay in insisting the Incarnation pertained to one person only, Jesus of Nazareth. The thesis of the present essay is that Christianity's original sin is to think it is about God.

David Strauss: A Protreptic

Strauss' program unfolds in two steps, the critique of history followed by the critique of dogma. Why the two? Strauss saw himself not just as a critical historian but above all as a *theologian* who reflects on the Jesus of history and the Christ of faith inasmuch as these two issues can be distinguished in the Gospels. The subject matter of his cri-tique was never the Gospels merely as texts presenting the (true or false) history of Jesus of Nazareth but always as texts embodying early Christian faith-affirmations, from "Jesus is Lord and Christ" in the Synoptics to "Jesus is God incarnate" in the Gospel of John. That latter and normatively orthodox sentence is made up of the subject, "the historical Jesus," and the predicate, "God incarnate." Strauss, as a theologian, had to make sense of both the historical and the doctrinal, which means that he had to train his critical guns on both elements of that affirmation.

In analyzing the subject of the sentence (a task that takes up most of his book) Strauss asks whether the New Testament stories about Jesus' supernatural deeds are historical or not. Here he attempts to separate out the bed-rock historical events of the life of Jesus from subsequent mythical and legendary faith-extrapolations — the same task that the Jesus Seminar has long and famously carried out.

However, Strauss argues that doing only this much is not enough. Despite the historical critique of the Gospels, the myths live on as received dogma and find a refuge in the souls of believers as objects of faith. That is why Strauss feels compelled to take the next step and focus his criticism no longer on the allegedly historical data of the Gospels but now on the presumed supernatural meaning of the data. In the concluding fifty-eight pages of the book ("Concluding Treatise: The Dogmatic Meaning of the Life of Jesus"[4]) Strauss no longer asks whether the Gospel stories accurately record miraculous supernatural happenings (he has already argued that they do not). He asks instead what meaning those stories — radically reinterpreted, of course — might still hold for Christians in his own day. Hence, from the "critique of history" to the "critique of dogma."

Strauss' critique of dogma does not intend to destroy the content of faith but to question its unquestionedness and retrieve from it the latent truth it harbors. Such a critique, he says, appears to be — and in fact is — negative, but not because it seeks to annihilate Christianity. The negativity is that of a Hegelian dialectic. Precisely in order to retrieve the still viable truth of Christian faith, Strauss must attack the "immediacy" of Christian faith, by which he means holding to beliefs intuitively and naively, without questioning, unfolding, and thus adequately comprehending them; in a word, without "mediating" belief through understanding.

> Against the immediacy of dogma, as against any immediacy, criticism has to arise in the form of negativity and the struggle for mediation. Now the critique is longer that of history, as

heretofore, but of dogma; and only when faith passes through both critiques has it been truly mediated, i.e., has it become knowledge.[5]

To carry out merely the critique of history, Strauss says, is to fail to achieve the complete understanding required of a responsible Christian. It is not just that the critique of history leaves us with the subject of the sentence bereft of a usable predicate — the Jesus of history without contemporary relevance — but that without the critique of dogma we might end up presuming a set of predicates about the meaning of Jesus, based on unclarified philosophical and theological presuppositions. For an intellectually responsible theologian — one who emphasizes the *logos* in theology, the *understanding* of faith — the critique of the Jesus of history inevitably entails the critique of the Christ of faith. The critique of faith is not an optional add-on but, in Strauss' words, "the ultimate object" of the critique of history.[6]

What is it that brings people like David Strauss, and us, to the point where we cannot avoid re-interpreting the contemporary relevance of the Jesus of history? What generates the perceived need for a radical hermeneutics that almost inevitably rattles the cage of traditional orthodoxy? Strauss offers a phenomenological description of how one might come to that point.[7]

The need for radical hermeneutics, he says, arises from an acute sense of crisis, a feeling not just of one's distance from the ancient texts but, more importantly, of the discrepancy between the spirit and culture of the New Testament and that of one's own world and culture. At first one notices the distance and discrepancy only in incidental matters: we do not understand a certain biblical expression or a specific cultural practice mentioned in the New Testament. In this way we tend to overlook just how radical the crisis is, and we continue to muddle through.

But eventually, he says, we see clearly that the discrepancy pertains to the essential content of the New Testament and that its fundamental ideas are in fact radically incommensurate with today. The immediate intervention of God in history and human affairs comes to seem improbable, perhaps even repellent. We end up denying that divine events could have happened the way the New Testament alleges and affirming that whatever did happen could not have been divine. In short, we reject the historical validity of the Bible and explain away what Strauss calls "the absolute content" of faith that is presented in these texts.

One response would be to blissfully deny the crisis, whether out of ignorance or bad faith, and "close our eyes," as Strauss says, "to one's own awareness of the discrepancy" between the world of the New Testament and our world today.[8] Such denial remains the default position in many of the Christian churches, certainly in a good deal of preaching and catechesis but even in some high-level scholarship that occasionally seems to encourage a schizoid embrace of cognitive dissonance in order to save the phenomena. One is reminded of what one prominent exegete has written about the possible discrepancy between the findings of history and the affirmations of Christian faith:

> [T]he Catholic approach has one advantage — the clear distinction between what is known through historical research and reason and what is affirmed in faith. The historical Jesus belongs solely to the former realm. Moreover, for a Catholic, what is affirmed in faith does not rest on the Bible alone; church tradition, official teaching and theological development all play a part. Consequently, my faith in Christ does not rise or fall on my fragmentary hypothetical reconstruction of Jesus through historical research.[9]

Such convenient distinctions between subject and predicate may well lend believers temporary shelter in the hurricane now ripping through Christianity, but one wonders how much longer this lean-to can last. Strauss' option was quite different — not to seek refuge in the accumulation of Christian tradition, ecclesiastical pronouncements, and theological speculations, but simply to face into the storm: "to unequivocally acknowledge and openly avow that the issues narrated in [the New Testament] have to be viewed in an entirely different light from that in which their authors regarded them." He calls for a radical salvage effort by way of a new hermeneutic that will hold to the essential while surrendering the nonessential.[10]

From the beginning, the Jesus Seminar has self-consciously taken its stand, as did Strauss in his times, at the center of the hermeneutical storm that defines contemporary culture, historical science, and thus Jesus-research. However, until recently and for good reasons, the Seminar has focussed almost exclusively on the critique of history rather than engaging the critique of dogma. But even apart from that, there are two important differences between Strauss' program and that of the Jesus Seminar.

First, Strauss was entirely forthcoming about his religious position — something that is much more difficult for the Seminar, since its many members hold such diverse beliefs in this regard. Second and more important, Strauss was completely candid about the philosophical presuppositions undergirding his critique of dogma. This was particularly true with regard to his "speculative Christology," which argued that the incarnation of God was not a one-time, one-person event but took place from all eternity and within the entire human species. Strauss' philosophical presuppositions were, of course, Hegelian and no doubt are uncongenial to most researchers today. But it would be erroneous to think that the members of the Jesus Seminar operate without any philosophical presuppositions guiding both their historical work and, to the degree they chose to follow Strauss's twofold program, their critique of dogma as well.

The Kingdom of God: A Sermon

In the service of the critique of dogma that makes up the second step of Strauss' program, I wish to sketch out some of the presuppositions that guide my own position on this matter. This will be only a sketch and no more: I will not lay out the arguments supporting those views (any more than Strauss did for his presuppositions in *Das Leben Jesu*). Rather, I would simply like to enact them in the form of a popular sermon (the way Strauss enacted his in the conclusion to his treatise), that is, put them to work while discussing what the future of Jesus' message might be. This sermon, unlike others that one might hear, is meant less to convince anyone — it is only one possible reading of the the message of Jesus — than to raise questions about how presuppositions work and what they can do.

In the sermon that follows I shall stay within what some theologians call the "anthropocentric paradigm," which follows out the dynamism of human spirit towards the possibility of its ultimate fulfillment. The first principle of such an approach is that, in second-order reflections on the possible relation of God to human beings (and a sermon is such a reflection), we must begin with ourselves, not with God — because there is no other place for us to begin. By the nature of the case, God is not an on-hand, readily available entity; if we believe in God and think we have been touched by him, it is *we* who believe in him and claim to have been touched by him. We relate to God from a human place and in a human way; and this is so even if we claim that we have known God through his self-communicating revelation.

In the name of asking what the message of Jesus might mean today, let us take a journey — "let us go, then, you and I" — and let us make it an "anthropocentric" journey, one that insists on remaining in the only place where we find ourselves and the only place where God, should he choose to do so, could reveal himself to us in Jesus: the human world of language and experience.

At the risk of being corny, I will make this journey be a train ride. This train will be making regular stops along the way, where you can get off whenever you have had enough. As we travel between stations, I will sketch out one possible anthropocentric approach to the question of God and his revelation in Jesus. After each such segment of the journey I will announce an up-coming station at which you are free to get off the train — but please don't forget to take all your baggage with you.

Finite infinity

The train slowly pulls out of the station. The first segment of the journey is about finite infinity.

One of the most fundamental and arguably obvious facts about human being and human consciousness is that they — that is, we — are radically finite. This might seem unproblematic enough; but there is a slight paradox here. Once one establishes the radical *finitude* of human being, one likewise establishes its radical *infinity*. However, this paradox can be easily resolved by distinguishing two kinds of infinity. On the one hand there is the infinity of God, who has everything together: he knows everything, controls everything, and has endless power. God's infinity entails that he does not have to do anything, to work at anything, to search for anything. As perfectly self-identical or coincident with himself — as Aristotle put it, an act of thinking that thinks of nothing other than of itself as an act of thinking: *noesis noeseos* — God already has everything. We may call this infinity a "perfect" or "good" infinity.

Human beings, on the other hand, precisely because they are not God, do not have everything together. They have to search and question, they need to learn things and work to control them. And because they never will have everything together, they must search and question and learn endlessly, that is to say, *infinitely*. Of themselves, these efforts are never over and done with. Like a mathematical infinity, you can always add one more on to the series, and one more again, endlessly, or at least until death. We can call this endless or imperfect infinity a "bad" infinity.

Whereas God's perfect infinity means that he is perfectly self-contained without losing or excluding anything that exists, our imperfect infinity means that we are never complete and closed in upon ourselves but, within the limits of our finitude and mortality, always open, always able to become more. This constitutes the "up-side" of imperfect infinity: we are open to everything, able to question, be interested in, and search for everything, able in principle to know something about everything, even if we never fully possess everything. This is what Aristotle was affirming centuries ago when he declared that the human *psyche* or soul "is in some way all things."[11]

We may envision the unfolding of human knowing as a progression through the world of whatever there is, in the direction of an ever-receding horizon. With every step forward in knowing and managing this or that, with every new acquisition within the world of the graspable and doable, the horizon moves backwards, opening up an even broader vista of what we can know and do. Thus, in principle we have access to and contact with everything in the world, even if only by questioning it. We are open to the endless intelligibility and accessibility of everything. And as we go forward, we never hit a final unsurpassable limit except our death. Not even the existence of God puts restraints on human capabilities.

Likewise with every step forward, we transcend our previous selves, and yet always bring those transcended selves along with us as our inheritance (what we have been and still are) even as we transcend ourselves again. In short, we are ever becoming ourselves without ceasing to be ourselves. Another name for our finite infinity is endless self-transcendence bordered only by our finitude and mortality.

This affirmation of the human being's finite infinity and endless self-transcendence contrained only by its intrinsic limitations is an affirmation of radical humanism, even if that is a de-centered humanism, a way of being human that is ever projected beyond itself into a future that never completely arrives. There is nowhere in the universe of being where we are not at home. The Latin motto "Nothing human is foreign to me" (*humani nil a me alienum*) becomes simply "Nothing at all is foreign to humans" (*ab homine nil alienum*). So too there is no tree in the Garden of Eden whose fruit we cannot eat. And if there is some fruit we should not eat, that is not because of a heteronomous command from the God beyond, but only because eating it would harm or constrict our finite infinity. The only sin is to refuse to be the mortal, finite, and thus endlessly self-transcending infinity that we are. In principle there is nothing we cannot know and manage endlessly (and in principle completely), unbounded by divine restrains. There is no way in which God's perfect infinity could ever function as a brake on our finite infinity — and this is not because of some hubristic defiance of God's creative power but owing to the very gift of that power.

We are pulling in to the second station. All those who object (understandably!) to this admittedly sketchy notion of finite infinity and radical humanism may want to get off here — but please don't forget your baggage. Among those who choose to disembark might be all who insist on putting an in-principle limit upon the human ability to know something about everything, and to have access to everything about anything in a mortal but infinite odyssey of intellect and will. Also, all off who think God has to be the final restraint on our finite infinity, that he is the wall we eventually will hit. However, those who believe in creation may want to stay on board since, on one account at least, that doctrine is precisely the tracks on which this train is running.

The ever-receding horizon

All aboard who are staying on for the next leg of the journey. The train pulls out of the second station. Next topic: the *goal* of infinite infinity.

Within the anthropocentric paradigm as I understand it, one of the jobs of philosophy is to figure out the correlate of our finite infinity, the objective or goal of our human striving. The correlate of human knowing is the humanly knowable, the correlate of human desiring is the humanly desirable. But what is the correlate of human becoming as a whole? What is the ultimate objective of the human odyssey?

In the traditional version of this correlation, the final objective of human becoming is God. Think of St. Augustine's *Confessions*: "You made us for yourself, O Lord, and our heart is restless until it rests in you."[12] In this view, the troubled journey of the soul will some day end in the quieting embrace of God — in fact, our restlessness has already begun to end, if only by way of anticipation. We are already proleptically at the end of our journey and in God's embrace, but not yet fully. And the tradition would insist that these are ontological facts that in principle can be established not just by revelation and faith but by philosophical reason alone, without supernatural aid or information.

In the vision that I propose, however, all we can affirm phenomenologically, that is, experientially, is this: Every step we take forward is answered by the horizon moving a step backward. If human being is endlessly open, then its correlate is the endlessly open-ended. It is not that human beings face toward a vaguely glimpsed God who awaits us up ahead, just beyond the end of the world. (To say this is not to deny that God exists but to deny that the "up-ahead" model is an adequate way to speak of God.) Rather, we face endless possibilities of self-realization within the world, in a progression bordered finally only by death as the end of our world.

As we face an endlessly receding horizon and thus the inexhaustible possibilities of human knowing and doing, there is no guarantee that the horizon, as it backs up, will hit some wall behind it (God, let us say) and stop receding. No, we never hit the wall. (Our dying is not a matter of hitting a wall but of just dying.) All we perform are endless acts of self-transcendence; and in that way we endlessly "humanize" the world, learning to be at home everywhere within it. In fact, if improbably we were to reach the horizon, the point where there was nothing more in the world to be known because we had come to know every worldly thing in its complete intelligibility, this would be no guarantee that we are now shouldering up against God, at least not the God of Jesus of Nazareth.

If you have had enough of this, you may want to consider switching trains at the up-coming station. There will be another one pulling in on track two, and on that train they believe that the constant receding of the horizon is the action of the hidden God, who, as he recedes, calls us forward into his final mysterious presence. As T. S. Eliots put it in *Four Quartets*:

> With the drawing of this Love and the voice of this Calling
> We shall not cease from exploration
> And the end of all our exploring
> Will be to arrive where we started
> And know the place for the first time.[13]

This beautiful poetic vision of the human odyssey weaves together the notions of Aristotle's God as final cause, Plotinus' return of the soul to its source, and Augustine's God of homecoming. However, it is a different journey from the one on this train.

We are pulling into the third station now — and there it is! — the T. S. Eliot Express over on Track 2, ready to take off in what seems to be the same direction as ours.

If you transfer to the T. S. Eliot Express you will soon notice that the people on that train apparently have an advantage over us. Over there they believe that the correlate of our finite infinity is the hidden God who stands beyond the horizon, drawing us onwards towards himself. The passengers over there are able to have it both ways. They get history now and eternity later; they operate on faith during the journey but attain to the vision of God once they pull into the final station. Most importantly they think that their train, while being governed to some extent by the secondary causality of nature, science, and technology (Newton's laws of motion, diesel power, and so forth), is ultimately being pulled to its final destination not by the secondary causality of the locomotive up front but by the final causality of God up ahead.

And over here on this train? No, we are not going in the same direction to the same final station. And no, the difference between this train and the T. S. Eliot Express is not that they know the final correlate of their movement to be God whereas we are undecided whether the correlate of our movement is God or the endless humanization of the world.

No, on this train we are not confused about our goal. Rather, we know that the goal we are moving towards is not God but more of our finitely infinite selves. The endless open-endedness that is the correlate of our self-transcendence is really our own territory, not God's; it is the realm of our own possibilities. You may want to call the receding of the horizon a mystery, but it is the mystery of ourselves as finite infinity. What the receding horizon makes available to us is our world; and what constitutes the receding of the horizon is our own finitude — not God, or God's drawing power, or our alleged progressive itinerary toward God. (Nor will we settle for some facile undecidability between "God" and "justice." We know the difference between the two. To say this is not to deny that God exists but to deny that the God-or-justice-take-your-pick model is a responsible way to think about God's relation to us.)

Our finite infinity means we are always a lack of fullness. We may try forever to fill up the lack, but we will never succeed: it's an abyss. To cover over that endless lack with the face of the distant God, or to hope it will be finally filled with the presence of the parousial God, would be only the last example of Bonhoeffer's God-of-the-gaps. In the final analysis our endlessness bespeaks not God but our present mortality and our future death; and to fill in that emptiness with God would be to deny our mortality. It would be the final blasphemy: "You certainly will not die: you will be like gods" (Gen 3:4, 5).

Rather, we should celebrate that lack as the form of our lives, as what gives us whatever measure of being we have. Why hope and pray

for rescue from it? God is not the final filling-in of our lack, the ultimate supplement that completes our finitude, because, by the very laws
of our creation, our lack cannot be filled and our finitude can have no
supplement. Thus it is out of a deep sense of piety in the divine creator
that we should refuse the name of God — much less the name "Abba"
— for that emptiness.

Last chance to disembark and transfer to the T. S. Eliot Express,
especially if you get motion-sick just thinking that the horizon keeps
receding as we move ahead and that this train will never reach a final
destination. All aboard who are staying aboard.

Long day's journey into co-openness

Looking around as we pull out of the station, I can see there are
very few of us left on the train. Most of our fellow passengers did transfer to the T. S. Eliot Express (let's hope they took their baggage with
them). So as the remaining few of us, the *anawim*, pull out of the station on the final, unconcluding leg of this journey, we may want to col-
lect our thoughts about where we are going and why we are still
together.

Despite the beauty, comfort, and assured destination of the Eliot
Express — the train of the God-up-ahead, drawing us onwards as he
recedes into mystery — there are a few reasons for declining to ride it.

The first reason is that the Eliot Express has gotten it all wrong
about the directionality of human vision. (That is why Thomas Aquinas
is still riding with us on this train and not on the other one.) Over there
they promise us an illusory metaphysical glimpse into the Beyond as a
supplement to our ordinary vision of this world — something that
Aquinas has shown to be impossible. He argues conclusively that we
human beings have only one legitimate line of vision, the view that our
senses have of this world of physical data, which we make sense of by
means of our spiritual faculties. According to Aquinas we cannot look
over and beyond sense data — cannot, as it were, stick our heads out
the train window and peer up ahead into the metaphysical future, catch
a glimpse of God waiting for us at the final station — and then return,
assured and comforted, to our seats and to our normal vision of the
world.

On this train, no hanging out the window to get a view up
ahead, no metaphysical vision added on as a supplement to our worldly
knowledge of things, no deep-back-up certitude that our train is
heaven-bent. Likewise, no double vision whereby we (1) love the God
who awaits us at the end of the line and then, for his sake, (2) love the

neighbor sitting next to us on the train. Not two visions, two loves, two movements, the one directed beyond towards God, the other directed back into the world. That may work on Plato's train or T. S. Eliot's but not on this one. Here you face only the physical things of this world, and you make intellectual and spiritual sense of them only within the ever-expanding horizon of human possibilities. Everything else lies outside your range of vision and is not covered by your ticket.

There is a second reason for not switching trains. Not only is it true that the horizon keeps receding, but we can never peer beyond it. And least of all should we ever attempt a leap of faith over it — because we would only land in nothing. Our horizon is like that of the expanding universe that keeps offering us more world to explore; but we cannot reach ahead and touch some "membrane" that defines the edge of the universe of experience, much less cut through it and penetrate to the other side — because there is no such "membrane" and there is no "other side," only more and more of this side. In fact, in the normal course of events we do not even look directly at the horizon. Instead we mostly tend to forget it, and rightly so. Apart from rare moments of what Plato and Aristotle called "wonder," we usually see the finitude of things on this side of the horizon rather than any finitizing darkness on the other side of things.

If you tried to pierce through the horizon, you would get caught up in a cyclone that hurls you back into this world and lands you right here among the rest of us finite self-transcenders. You can no more peer beyond the horizon than you can climb inside your own consciousness, for the nature of both of them, the horizon and your consciousness, is to rebound you back into the world. The mystery of the ever-receding horizon is about more of yourself beyond yourself; and the job of that ever-receding horizon is to give you more of this world, this realm of meaning, these things, this life.

The third and most important reason for refusing to change trains — that is, for declining to say that the correlate of our finite infinity is the God who draws us on as he recedes — is that it is very dangerous.

Consider this: The fact that our ultimate correlate is an ever-receding horizon (and the correspondingly ever-expanding world of human knowing and doing) means that we are not God (God has no horizon and needs no world), we are not perfect, complete, and already in possession of everything. Unlike God, none of us is a self-contained unit; each of us is extended and plural, not the whole of humanity but always a part of the human whole. By our very nature as finite infinity we are social, not atomistic (much less Adam Smith-istic) but always one of the species without losing our singularity, inevitably part of a multitude that lives in common, each one of us bound to all the others and to the common good, no one of us ever finally free or fulfilled until the whole community is free and fulfilled.

The ever-receding horizon bespeaks not only the generic "radical humanism" that we mentioned above but also and more specifically a radically *social* humanism. Our endless co-openness — our sociality or "species-being," as some have put it — is never an add-on to an otherwise atomistic self, sufficient unto itself. Instead, our sociality and how we relate to it defines our individuality.

But notice some consequences. If the ever-receding horizon bespeaks endless possibilities for realizing our human powers in the world, limited only by mortality, and if our openness is always social co-openness, then what we are moving towards in self-transcendence is social self-realization, perhaps asymptotic but nonetheless an immanent rather than a transcendent realization.

This is why it is dangerous for those who are riding the T.S. Eliot Express to call the correlate of human becoming "God." For if one does choose to use the word "God" to name the open-ended correlate of human openness, then "God" would be a name for the perhaps asymptotic but nonetheless immanent fulfillment of the whole human species across history. The word "God" would be a marker for the full unfolding of all the natural and social powers of humankind. Then we really would be in bed with David Strauss, along with Hegel, Feuerbach, and Marx, and wouldn't that be fun. . . .

Now a thought-experiment: What if, while still declining to ride the Eliot Express, we nonetheless chose to call the correlate of our social co-open-endedness by the name "God"?

A first thought: In this vale of tears, what really needs love and care and reassurance, what really requires respect and attention, is not God (who is doing quite well, thank you) but humankind. Wouldn't it be bizarre to think of God as some neurotic Roman Emperor who is forever getting annoyed when he fails to get enough attention? No, it is human beings who need nurturing, attention, respect, and fulfillment; and they deserve that for their own sake, not as a second-order reflux from another's love of God, and not as a mere stepping stone towards some higher good.

A second thought: Can we imagine the following? What if God, without reserve and without expectation of return, were to lend his name as a stand-in for, and a protection of, the intrinsic and unending fulfillment of the human community? What if God allowed his name to be used for the open-ended correlate of our socially co-open infinity?

If that were so, then on our train the word "God" would name the possibility of the asymptotic unfolding of our social powers precisely as immanent natural powers. The word "God" would hold open that space of possibility for social self-realization and would protect it against the ever encroaching forces of dehumanization that seek to reduce us to something less than our full social freedom, to make us into (for example) mere consumers, or bean-counters, or "profit-maximizing animals," or the like. If God did lend his name for this purpose — without reserve and without expectation of return — then in saving the name of God we would be saving ourselves.

But we would also have finally lost the God up ahead and up above, the Supreme Being who, even after the Incarnation, continues to rule history from beyond the world, who reveals himself from his supernatural heaven, and then draws us, as he drew his only begotten Son, onwards, upwards, and outwards to our transcendent fulfillment.

It is not that we declare, out of pride or hubris, that we have outgrown our need of the traditional God, no longer find him useful, but rather that the very meaning of "God" would have revealed itself to be *kenosis*, a self-emptying self-communicating God poured out without remainder, not clinging to the form of a transcendent divinity but emptying himself into the form of finite infinity, happily dying as transcendent in order to be reborn in the endless mortal struggle to live our co-openness in common, to endlessly enhance each other, to humanize nature and naturalize the human — not for any transcendent divine motive but for no other reason than itself.

If (continuing the thought-experiment) we can at least imagine God might do that, then to what would we liken the kingdom of God? It would be not a gift *from* God but the gift *of* God entirely given over without remainder. Not the hypostatic incarnational union of the divine and human natures coming together from opposite poles of the ontological universe, but the end of the need and ability to make such distinctions.

But surely that could not be the kingdom of God! Doesn't the kingdom require a transcendent Abba, all powerful, who gives us our daily bread, forgives our sins, whose will shall someday be done on earth as it is in heaven, when his kingdom comes? Or could the kingdom of God be the end of transcendence, the end of "God" and the beginning of co-open-endedness, which means our resolute living in common for justice and mercy?

But what a labor this would be to reinterpret every category and attribute of "God" as a marker of our infinite co-openness! and above all, to take the highest name for God — the Holy, the Blessèd One — and read it instead as "making holy, making blessèd" — in a word, "anointing" — such that the title *meshiah* or *christos*, "the anointed and blessed," would become an ontological designation of our finite infinity, and such that the doing of justice and mercy would become (to use the name the early Christians used for their way of living) the holy and blessed Way.

What then would faith be? Would it mean believing the unbe-lievable? holding to propositions that we cannot fully comprehend? Or might it be trust in and commitment to the endless tasks of justice and mercy without need of transcendent motivations or sanctions? What would hope be? A yearning for the end of history and the fulfillment of our final fantasy of living forever in God's heaven as pure, post-mortem souls with eternal consciousness? Or might it be hope against hope in the unending struggle for human justice and mercy on this side of death? And what would love be? Would it be that double-visioned love of the transcendent God and worldly human beings, the latter for the sake of the former? Or would that distinction disappear?*

And the Jesus of history? What would any of this have to do with him? Imagine that only half of what we know of the Jesus of his-tory were true: common table fellowship, overturning the dominant social hierarchy, consorting with outcasts, challenging the empire and the religious establishment. Then postulate that Jesus somehow found out that he had no Abba in heaven who gives us our daily bread, for-gives our sins, and promises to realize his heavenly kingdom on earth. On that premise, can you imagine Jesus giving it up, throwing it all over, eating only with the rich, joining the conservative establishment, reaffirming the old hierarchies, kissing the wrist of Rome? Did Jesus' message of the kingdom stand or fall with his faith in the transcendent God?

We cannot speak for him, of course, and the question might even seem foolish and trivial, perhaps even offensive. But what is not foolish and trivial (though it may turn out to be offensive) is what we know we must do, based on what we think we are and where we think we are going.

---

*Is it possible that those who have learned something from Jesus' message of the kingdom of God might choose to celebrate sacraments and liturgies, eucharists and feasts, to solemnize the mystery of endless co-openness? Could the churches ever be what Nietzsche called them, "the tombs and sepulchers of God," but now in a positive sense: the temples of justice and mercy?

The sermon is over. As I promised, it has been nothing more than a very idiosyncratic enactment one set of presuppositions. The intent is not to convince anyone to share these presuppositions but to suggest that each of us has some such story, a proto-anthropology and a proto-theology, mostly unthematized, which guides his or her interpretation of Jesus' message. The future of that message will depend in good measure on how we clarify our views on human being and its relation to its final end, and use them to reinterpret the kingdom of God.

Notes

1. In Origen's commentary on the Gospel of Matthew, *Patrologia Graeca* XIII (1862), p. 1197.
2. David Friedrich Strauss, *Das Leben Jesu kritisch bearbeitet*, Tübingen: C. F. Osiander, vol. 1, 1835; vol. 2, 1836. On the title page of volume 2 Strauss is identified as "Dr. der Philos. und Repeteten am evangelisch-theologischen Seminar zu Tübingen" and the volume ironically bears the *imprimatur* "Mit Königl. Würtembergischem Privilegium gegen den Nachdruck"! The fourth edition of the work (1839) was brought into English as *The Life of Jesus Critically Examined*, translated by George Eliot (Mary Ann Evans), three volumes, London: Chapman Brothers, 1846. Eliot's translation, edited and introduced by Peter C. Hodgson, has been republished under the same title, in a one-volume edition, by Philadelphia: Fortress Press, 1972. In this essay I follow the first German edition, with its often idiosyncratic spellings.
3. "Den inneren Kern des christlichen Glaubens weiss der Verfasser von seinen kritischen Untersuchungen völlig unabhängig. Christi übernatürliche Geburt, seine Wundern, seine Auferstehung und Himmelfahrt, bleiben ewige Wahrheiten, so sehr ihre Wirklichkeit als historischer Fakta angezweifelt werden mag. . . .Den dogmagtischen Gehalt des Lebens Jesu wird eine Abhandlung am Schlusse des Werkes als unversehrt aufzeigen. . . ." *Das Leben Jesu*, "Vorrede," 1: vii–viii.
4. "Schlussabhandlung. Die dogmatische Bedeutung des Lebens Jesu," *Das Leben Jesu*, 2:686–744.
5. "Erwacht daher allerdings auch gegen das in seiner Unmittelbarkeit auftretende Dogma, wie gegen jede Unmittelbarkeit, die Kritik als Negativität und Streben nach Vermittlung: so ist diese doch nicht mehr, wie bisher, historische, sondern dogmatische Kritik, und erst durch beide hindurchgegangen, ist der Glaube wahrhaft vermittelt, oder zum Wissen geworden." *Das Leben Jesu*, 2:688.
6. "ihr leztes Ziel," *Das Leben Jesu*, 2: 689.
7. *Das Leben Jesu*, 1:2.
8. "wenn sie gegen das Bewusstsein der Differenz zwischen der neuen Bildung und der alten Urkunde sich verblendet," *Das Leben Jesu*, 1:2.
9. John P. Meier, *New York Times Book Review*, December 21, 1986, p. 16.
10. Cf. " . . . wenn sie klar erkennt und offen eingesteht, dass sie das, was jene alten Schriftsteller erzählen, anders ansieht, als diese selbst es angesehen haben. Dieser letztere Standpunkt ist jedoch keineswegs schon ein Sichlossagen von den alten Religionsschriften, sondern es kann auch hier noch bei Festhaltung des Wesentlichen das Unwesentliche ungescheut preissgegeben werden." *Das Leben Jesu*, 1:2–3.
11. Aristotle, *On the Soul*, 3. 2 431b21 (*he psyche ta onta pos esti panta*); and Thomas Aquinas, *De veritate*, qu. I, art. 1, responsio, in Thomas Aquinas

in *Quaestiones de veritate* (in *Quaestiones disputatae et quaestiones duodecim quodlibetales*, 3–5 [Turin and Rome: Marietti, 1942]), p. 3A (*quod natum est convenire cum omni ente*).

12. "Tu excitas, ut laudare te delectet, quia fecisti nos ad te et inquietum est cor nostrum, donec requiescat in te." *Confessiones* 1.1.

13. T. S. Eliot, "Little Gidding," V, (Four Quartets), *The Complete Poems and Plays of T. S. Eliot* (London: Faber and Faber, 1969), p. 197.

Marcus J. Borg

Re-visioning Christianity

I am grateful for the invitation to speak to you as we celebrate the work of the Jesus Seminar and engage in reflecting together about "The Once and Future Jesus." I do so as both a Fellow of the Jesus Seminar and a Christian.

By profession I am a historian of the Bible specializing in the study of Jesus and Christian origins. By confession and commitment, I am a Christian. As such, I was nurtured in the Lutheran tradition and remained Lutheran until about age thirty. For much of my thirties, I dropped out of church altogether, even though the Bible, Jesus and Christian origins continued to be my object of study and my abiding intellectual fascination. At around age forty, I re-entered the life of the church as an Episcopalian. I now describe myself as a committed Christian of a non-literalistic and non-exclusivistic kind.

Today I speak to you primarily as a Christian who is also a biblical scholar. I will talk about the significance for the church of the kind of work we do as biblical scholars. In particular, I will argue that contemporary biblical and Jesus scholarship is playing a central role in a major development occurring within mainline churches in North America. In shorthand, I call that that development a "re-visioning of Christianity." I see my primary Christian vocation as "midwifery": assisting the birthing process of this re-visioning of Christianity underway in our time.

And hence the title of my talk: "Re-visioning Christianity at the Millennium." My starting point: I am convinced that an older way of seeing Christianity has come undone for many people over the last thirty to forty years. This older understanding nourished the lives of millions of Christians for hundreds of years. But it has ceased to be persuasive to many people in our time, especially among the

45

demographic groups from whom mainline churches typically have drawn their members.

I am also convinced that there is widespread hunger for a new way of seeing Christianity, a "re-visioning." Indeed, I think this hunger accounts for the remarkable public response to the Jesus Seminar (and Jesus scholarship generally). Of course, what we do is interesting. But the response would not be so great if there were not a strong grass-roots desire among both laity and clergy in mainline churches for a way of seeing Christianity that makes persuasive and compelling sense.

And thus a major need for the mainline church as the millennium draws to a close is a thoughtful re-visioning of foundational elements of Christian theology. Indeed, though there may be more important humanitarian and justice issues, I think this is the most important theological task of our time. What is at stake is both the credibility of Christianity and our vision of the Christian life: what is it most centrally about?

An important clarification: when I speak of "re-visioning," there is a meaning of that word I do not intend. Namely, we sometimes use the word "revision" to mean that a term paper or manuscript needs a lot of editing, perhaps even needs to be re-done. That's not what I mean. Rather, I mean re-visioning in the sense of "seeing again." Thus I consistently use a hyphen between "re" and "visioning": I will be speaking about seeing the Christian tradition again.

As I do so, I will describe two different ways of seeing the Christian tradition, two versions or two visions of the Christian life: an older conventional understanding and one that is now coming into view. Both are present in the church today. They are two comprehensively different ways of envisioning the Christian tradition and what it means to be a Christian as the twentieth century and the second millennium draw to a close.

As I conclude this introduction, I want to emphasize that both are ways of seeing the tradition. It is not that the older way of seeing is the tradition, and the newer one an abandonment or rejection or reduction of the tradition. Rather, both are ways of seeing the tradition as a whole.

To provide you with a roadmap of my talk, there are three main parts. In part one, I provide a sketch of an older conventional way of seeing Christianity. In part two, I make some comments about why it has come undone. In part three, the longest section, I sketch the central elements of the re-visioning.

The Older Way of Seeing Christianity

The older understanding is what I (and many of us) grew up with. It was "common" or "conventional" Christianity as recently as a generation ago, and is still the common understanding among our fundamentalist and conservative Christian brothers and sisters. I will describe this older way of seeing Christianity with five adjectives, explaining each with a brief exposition.

First, it was literalistic, in harder and softer forms. The hard form of literalism is, of course, fundamentalism: the insistence that the Bible and central Christian teachings are to be understood literally. But there is also a softer form of literalism, the kind that I grew up with. The Lutheran family and congregation in which I was nurtured were never very concerned about interpreting the Genesis stories of creation literally. We had no problem seeing the six days of creation as six geological epochs, and we didn't have to deny the existence of dinosaurs.

But we did take it for granted that the most important events in the Bible happened pretty much as they are described: that at the time of the exodus, the sea really did part to allow the ancient Hebrews to pass through; that Jesus really was born of a virgin, really did walk on the water, really did multiply loaves, and so forth. This is what I mean by a "softer" form of literalism: affirming the "happenedness" of the most central events.

Second, the older way of seeing Christianity was quite doctrinal. By this I mean simply that it was taken for granted that being a Christian meant believing central Christian doctrines to be true in a straightforward way. If you grew up in a church that used either the Apostles' Creed or Nicene Creed regularly, it meant being able to say the creed without crossing your fingers or becoming silent during any of the phrases.

Third, it was quite moralistic, by which I mean two things. The first: being a Christian was about being "good," and being good meant trying to live in accord with the ethical teaching of Scripture. That teaching could be understood as a narrow and highly specific code of righteousness, or more broadly as following general principles and ideals, such as the golden rule or loving your neighbor as yourself.

The second aspect of what I mean by "moralistic": we aren't very good at being good. Hence this older way of being Christian was centered on sin, guilt, and forgiveness. Indeed, it is striking how central the dynamic of sin and guilt has been. Most Christian worship services include a confession of sin and most eucharistic liturgies have sin and sacrifice at their center. Even quite liberal churches continue this emphasis. I was struck by this a few years ago when I spoke at a week-long conference in a liberal Christian setting. Each day began with a worship service that included a confession of sin after the opening hymn. I thought to myself, "It's nine o'clock in the morning, and we've already been bad."

Fourth, it was quite exclusivistic. In hard form, Christian exclusivism is the insistence that Jesus is the only way of salvation and Christianity the only true religion. There is also a softer form: feeling somewhat uncomfortable with the exclusivistic claim, but also feeling that it is a deeply traditional Christian claim, and that therefore one ought to believe it.

Fifth and finally, the older way of seeing Christianity was afterlife-oriented. "Where will you spend eternity?" was the crucial question in the form of Christianity I learned as a child. Indeed, a blessed afterlife was the primary meaning of "salvation": to be "saved" meant going to heaven, or being confident that you would when you died. So central was the afterlife to the understanding I received growing up in the church that if you had been able to convince me at age twelve or so that there was no afterlife, I would have had absolutely no idea why I should be a Christian. The afterlife was what it was all about.

Cumulatively, to put this older understanding into a single sentence: "Be a Christian now for the sake of salvation later." Or, to express the same notion in only slightly different words: "Believe in Christianity now for the sake of heaven later." And the emphasis was on "believing" — believing all of this to be true.

It is this way of seeing Christianity that has come undone over the past half century. For many in our time, there is a crisis of confidence about the Christian tradition. People have responded in a variety of ways. Many have left the church. As we all know, there has been a major decline in the membership of mainline denominations over the same period of time, and major growth of what Bishop John Spong calls "the church alumni association."

Some Christians vigorously defend the older understanding, and often claim that the reason for the decline of mainline denominations is that they have become soft about conventional Christian teachings. Still others remain within the church or on its margins, but are looking for a way of being Christian that makes persuasive and compelling sense to them.

Why the Older Understanding Has Come Undone

Why has this older way of seeing Christianity ceased to be persuasive? The primary reason: because of who we have become. I turn now to the second main point of my talk, namely, who we are at the millennium. And by "we," I mean "us," those of us gathered here today, and people who are part of mainline denominations and the demographic groups from whom they typically have drawn their members. Indeed, I mean most of us in modern western culture.

And so I will be making cultural generalizations about us on a grand scale. In particular, I will describe us with four statements. Though not a comprehensive description of who we have become, they name four factors that affect our view of life and religion and Christianity.

1. We are aware of religious pluralism. We are aware of the world's religions in a way that most people have not been for most of human history, even as recently as a century ago. We know about other religious traditions to varying degrees and in a variety of ways: from college religion courses, or our own reading, or public television series such as those featuring Joseph Campbell and Huston Smith, or from personal acquaintance with people of other traditions. This is simply part of our increasingly global awareness.

Thus for many of us, the exclusivistic claims of the Christian tradition are impossible to accept, both for "common sense" reasons and Christian theological reasons. Does it make sense that the creator of the whole universe would be known in only one religious tradition (which fortunately just happens to be our own)? Moreover, such a claim is difficult to reconcile with the centrality of "grace" in the Christian tradition. If one must be a Christian in order to be in right relationship with God, then there is a requirement, and we are no longer talking about grace.

2. We are aware of historical and cultural relativity. We are aware that how people think (including how we think) in a comprehensive sense is pervasively shaped by the time and place in which they live, as well as by social and economic class. When I say "in a

comprehensive sense," I mean our concepts, images, language, and thought processes: all of these are profoundly shaped by culture, by the total world in which people live.

And thus we are suspicious that any particular body of doctrines or teachings can be absolute truth or the only truth. It is all conditioned, relative to the time and place in which it originated. So also we are suspicious of attempts to exempt anything from this category, such as the Bible or the doctrines of our own tradition.

3. We are modern people, and as a result, we tend to be fact fundamentalists. My third statement about us is a compound sentence with two parts. To explain each part separately: when I say we are modern people, I mean simply that we live in the age of modernity. Modernity is that period of western history that began with the Enlightenment of the seventeenth century and continues into the present. Modernity is marked by scientific ways of knowing; indeed, the birth of modern science is also the birth of modernity.

Modernity is also marked by the modern world view (sometimes called the Newtonian world-view): what is real is that which can be known through scientific ways of knowing. Epistemology (how we know) became ontology (what is real). For the modern world-view, what is "real" is the space-time world of matter and energy. It is an image of reality as made up of tiny bits and pieces of "stuff," all of it interacting with each other in accord with "natural laws," producing a picture of the universe as a closed system of cause and effect. Importantly, the modern world-view has already been superceded in theoretical physics. But it continues to operate powerfully in our minds.

A major effect of modernity: we are preoccupied with factuality — with scientifically verifiable facts, and historically reliable facts. If a statement isn't scientifically or historically factual, it isn't true. Indeed, we live in the only culture in human history that has identified truth (and reality) with factuality. As a culture, we are "fact fundamentalists," a phrase I owe to Huston Smith.

Within the church, both fundamentalists and liberals have been preoccupied with factuality. For fundamentalists, the Bible must be factually true in order to be true at all (and hence their emphasis on the literal and historical factuality of biblical texts). Christian liberals have followed a different strategy: we have generally tried to rescue a few facts from the fire. But fundamentalists and liberals alike have agreed: facts are what matter.

This emphasis on factuality has had a pervasive and distorting effect on how we see the Bible and Christianity. One of the results is that Christianity in the modern period has been preoccupied with believing — that is, with believing "iffy" claims to be factually true. For many people, this has become the primary meaning of "faith" — as if what God most wants from us is to believe doubtful statements to be true.

4. We live on the boundary of post-modernity. At the end of the twentieth century, we are living in the frontier-land of a new period of cultural history that is dawning. We don't know what to call it yet, so we simply call it "post-modernity" (meaning "it's what comes next").

Post-modernity is a large and complex phenomenon. Moreover, some post-modern movements seem to me to be dead ends. Thus I will not attempt a comprehensive description (or even definition) of post-modernity, but will content myself with mentioning three characteristics of primary importance for our purposes.

Post-modernity is marked by the realization that modernity itself is a culturally-conditioned relative historical construction. The modern world-view is not the final word about reality, any more than previous constructions of reality have been the final word. Post-modernity knows that someday the Newtonian world-view will seem as quaint and archaic as the Ptolemaic world-view, a development that has already occurred among theoretical physicists.

Post-modernity is also marked by a turn to experience. In a time when traditional religious teachings have become suspect, we tend to trust that which can be known in our own experience. This turn to experience is seen in the remarkable resurgence of interest in spirituality within mainline churches and beyond. Spirituality is the experiential dimension of religion.

Finally, post-modernity is marked by a movement beyond fact fundamentalism to the realization that stories can be true without being literally and factually true. This development is reflected in much of contemporary theology's emphasis on metaphorical theology. To say the obvious, but it has so often been forgotten during the period of modernity: metaphors can be profoundly true, even if they are not literally or factually true.

Seeing Christianity Again: A Sketch of the Re-visioning

What would a form of Christianity look like that takes seriously both the Christian tradition and who we have become?

To summarize it negatively, it is to a large extent the opposite of the older understanding: not literalistic, not very doctrinal, not about being good for the sake of a reward later, not exclusivistic, not very much about believing, and not focused on an afterlife but on transformation in this life. To summarize it positively, I will speak of a relational and sacramental vision of the Christian life.

There are three foundational elements in the re-visioning: how we see God, Jesus, and the Bible. I will treat the first two very briefly. But the brevity should not be confused with being of less importance. Rather, the brevity is due in part to my having already said quite a bit about God and Jesus in print, and in part because of the importance of the third element, namely, how we see the Bible. I will then conclude with the vision of the Christian life that emerges from this way of seeing the foundational elements of the tradition.

Seeing God Again

The first foundational element concerns how we think about God (or "the sacred" or "Spirit," terms which I use synonymously and interchangeably).[1] We think about God with concepts and images. The most common concept of God in modern western Christianity sees God as a supernatural person-like being "out there." A long time ago, this God created the universe as something separate from God. From time to time, from "out there" God intervenes in the created order, especially in the more spectacular events reported in the biblical tradition, and perhaps even now. But most of the time God is not here, but "out there."

The shorthand phrase for this older conventional way of thinking about God is "supernatural theism." Supernatural theism has problems, however, and has become an intellectual obstacle to many in our time. They find it very difficult to believe in God as a person-like being "out there" who occasionally intervenes. What can it mean to be beyond a universe that we think of as enormous in size, maybe even infinite? And if God is thought of as sometimes intervening, how does one account for the non-interventions?

The re-visioning sees God very differently. The sacred is not distant and separate from the universe. Rather, God is the encompassing Spirit who is all around us, "right here," as well as "more" than right here. A number of theologians use the term "panentheism" to name this way of thinking about God.

Panentheism is quite different from pantheism, with which it is often confused. Its meaning is suggested by its Greek roots. The first syllable means "all" or "everything"; the middle syllable is a Greek preposition that means "in"; and the final syllable is from theos, the Greek word for "god." In short, panentheism means "everything is in God." Thus, for panentheism, the universe is not separate from God; rather, the universe is in God.

The change from supernatural theism to panentheism is not something new, but the recovery of something very old. To use semi-technical language to make the point: in the history of Christian thought, God has consistently been spoken of as both immanent and transcendent. Immanence affirms God's presence everywhere. Transcendence refers to God's "moreness" — that God is more than the universe, even as God is also everywhere present.

Supernatural theism affirms only the transcendence of God (and hence the concept of God as "out there," separate from and beyond the universe). Supernatural theism is thus wrong — wrong because it is incomplete. On the other hand, panentheism affirms both the immanence and transcendence of God. And because it affirms both, it is in fact the ancient and the orthodox voice of the Christian tradition.

Finally, the change from supernatural theism to panentheism matters. It matters not because God wants us to get our theology right, but it matters to us. It will affect our sense of the reality of God. As noted earlier, supernatural theism with its problems has become an intellectual obstacle to many people in our time. Panentheism does not have these problems. The change will also affect our sense of what prayer is about. Because supernatural theism makes God exceedingly far away, prayer can seem like calling into a universe that may be empty. Within panentheism, prayer is seen as addressing "the one in whom we live and move and have our being" (17.28), the sacred reality who is "right here" as well as "more" than right here.

Seeing Jesus Again

Because I have written much about Jesus, I will here content myself with emphasizing the importance of the distinction between the pre-Easter Jesus and the post-Easter Jesus.[2] The first phrase refers to the historical Jesus, a Galilean Jewish peasant of the first century, a figure of the past, dead and gone. He is nowhere anymore, a statement which does not deny Easter, but simply recognizes that the flesh and blood, corpuscular, protoplasmic Jesus is a figure of the past.

By "the post-Easter Jesus," I mean most simply what Jesus became after his death. More fully, I mean the Jesus of Christian experience and tradition. Both nouns are important. With the first noun, I refer to the risen living Christ of Christian experience. I take the phenomenology of Christian religious experience very seriously. From the first century onward and and continuing to today, some of his followers have had experiences of him as a figure of the present, and as a divine reality with the qualities of God.

With the second noun "tradition," I refer to the Jesus of the developing Christian tradition as found in the gospels, the New Testament as a whole, and the creeds. This Jesus is increasingly spoken of as a divine figure, climactically so in the Nicene Creed of the fourth century which speaks of him as very God of very God, of one substance with God, indeed as the second person of the Trinity.

Much is at stake in making the distinction between the pre- and post-Easter Jesus. When I was growing up in the church, I didn't know about the distinction, and so I lost both. I put everything I heard about Jesus into a single pot. And so I thought of the historical Jesus as already a divine figure — as the only begotten Son of God, even as the second person of the Trinity. I took it for granted that he had the mind of God (that's why he knew things) and the power of God (that's why he could do things like walking on the water, and so forth).

The result: I lost Jesus as a credible human being. A person who has the mind and power of God, who is the second person of the Trinity incarnate, is not flesh of our flesh and bone of our bones. Indeed, whenever we emphasize the divinity of Jesus at the expense of his humanity, we lose track of the utterly remarkable person he was. As the South African gospel scholar Albert Nolan puts it, "Jesus is a much underrated man. To deprive this man of his humanity is to deprive him of his greatness."[3]

Importantly, I also lost the living Christ of the present. For me, Jesus was a divine figure of the past who was here for awhile, thirty years more or less. Now, after his resurrection and ascension, he is with God and no longer here, though he will come again some day. But in the meantime, he is not around.

To conclude: when we do not make the distinction between the pre-Easter Jesus and the post-Easter Jesus, we risk losing both. When we do make the distinction, we get both — and both matter. And this is why historical Jesus scholarship is important: it helps us to see the distinction between the human Jesus and the divine Christ, and to glimpse the utterly remarkable person Jesus of Nazareth was.

Seeing the Bible Again

In the rest of this lecture, I focus on the Bible. I do so for two reasons. It is foundational for the Christian tradition; and confusion and conflict about the Bible is the central theological issue in the church in North America today. Conflict about the Bible is the major source of division between fundamentalist and conservative churches, on the one hand, and mainline denominations, on the other hand. Moreover, the conflict exists within the mainline denominations themselves.

The re-visioning of the Bible that I suggest has five points.

1. Seeing the Bible as a human product. To make the implicit contrast explicit, we need to see the Bible as a human product, not a divine product. It is easy to understand why the older conventional understanding saw the Bible as a divine product. In the Christian tradition, we have consistently spoken of it as "the Word of God" and "inspired by God," language which readily suggests that the Bible comes from God in a way that no other collection of writings does. Near the end of this lecture, I will suggest another way of understanding this language.

When I say the Bible is a human product, I mean simply that it is the product of two ancient communities. The Hebrew Bible (the Christian Old Testament) is the product of ancient Israel, and the New Testament is the product of the early Christian movement. As the product of these two communities, the Bible tells us about their life with God — about how they saw things and how they told their stories.

When we are not completely clear and candid about the Bible being a human product, we create the possibility of enormous confusion. I provide two quick illustrations of the difference it makes.

The first concerns the Genesis stories of creation. If we think of the Bible as a divine product, then these are God's stories of creation. As God's stories, they cannot be wrong. If we go very far down this road, we may find ourselves involved in scientific creationism and perhaps even in school board conflicts about whether Genesis should be taught alongside of evolution in public school biology courses. But if we think of the opening chapters of Genesis as ancient Israel's stories of creation, we realize that ancient Israel (like virtually every culture known to us) had its creation stories. And if we ask, "What are the chances that ancient Israel's stories of creation contain scientifically accurate information?" the answer would be, "About zero." And if they did, it would be sheer coincidence. Let me add that I think Israel's creation stories are profoundly true — but true as metaphorical or symbolic narratives, not as literally factual accounts.

The second illustration concerns the laws of the Bible. If we think of the Bible as a divine product, then the laws of the Bible are God's laws. To use one of the hot-button issues in the contemporary church to make the point, consider the single law in the Hebrew Bible prohibiting homosexual behavior between men. The prohibition is found in Lev 18:22, with the penalty (death) found two chapters later in Lev 20:13. If we think of the Bible as a divine product, then this is one of God's laws, and the ethical question becomes, "How can one justify setting aside one of the laws of God?"

But if we think of the Bible as a human product, then the laws of the Hebrew Bible are ancient Israel's laws, and the prohibition of homosexual behavior tells us that such behavior was considered unacceptable in ancient Israel. The ethical question then becomes, "What would be the justification for continuing to see this matter as ancient Israel did?" The question becomes even more acute when we realize that this law is embedded in a collection of laws that, among other things, prohibits planting two kinds of seed in the same field and wearing garments made of two kinds of cloth. How many of you are wearing blends today? My point is that we readily recognize some of these laws as the laws of an ancient culture which we are not bound to follow. Why then single out some as "the laws of God"?

2. Seeing the Bible as a combination of historical memory and metaphorical narratives. The meaning of "historical memory" is evident: some events reported in the Bible really happened, and the community preserved the memory of their having happened. The meaning of "metaphorical narratives" takes a bit longer to explain. They are of two kinds. Sometimes a historical event lies behind them, but the way the story is told gives it a metaphorical meaning as well. For example, ancient Israel did have her origin in the exodus from Egypt, but the way the story is told gives it metaphorical or symbolic meanings. Sometimes metaphorical narratives are purely metaphorical; that is, no particular historical event lies behind them (for example, the creation stories, the stories of Jesus walking on water and multiplying loaves).

It seems that the ancient communities which produced the Bible often metaphorized their history, and then we have often historicized their metaphors. To make the same point only slightly differently, they often mythologized their history, and then we have often literalized their mythology. But when one literalizes a metaphor, the result is nonsense. On the other hand, when one recognizes a metaphorical narrative as such, the result is a powerful story. This leads directly to my next point.

3. Seeing the Bible as stories about the divine-human relationship. The Hebrew Bible is ancient Israel's story of her relationship with God. The Christian Testament is the early Christian movement's story of her relationship with God as disclosed in Jesus.

Moreover, these stories are not just about the divine-human relationship in the past, but also in the present. A particularly illuminating way of making this point is with the way the exodus story is understood in the Jewish celebration of Passover each year. A liturgy accompanies the Passover meal, and it includes the following words (slightly paraphrased):

> It was not just our fathers and our mothers who were Pharaoh's slaves in Egypt, but we, all of us gathered here tonight, were Pharaoh's slaves in Egypt. And it was not just our fathers and mothers who were led out of Egypt by the great and mighty hand of God, but we, all of us gathered here tonight, were led out of Egypt by the great and mighty hand of God.

What is the meaning of this language? It does not mean that we were there in the loins of our ancestors, as if it were our DNA that was there. Rather, the exodus story is understood to be true in every generation. It portrays the human condition or predicament as bondage, and it proclaims that it is God's will that we be liberated from bondage. The story of Israel's bondage in Egypt and her liberation by God is a metaphor for the divine-human relationship.

4. Seeing the Bible in a state of post-critical naïveté. Given the above, a major need in the contemporary church is helping people move from pre-critical naïveté through critical thinking to post-critical naïveté. I turn now to explaining these three phrases.

Pre-critical naïveté is an early childhood state in which we take it for granted that whatever the significant authority figures in our lives tell us to be true is indeed true. To illustrate, I recall the way I heard the Christmas stories when I was a child. I took it for granted that the birth of Jesus really happened the way Matthew and Luke and our Christmas pageants portrayed it: that there really was a special star guiding the wisemen; that angels really sang in the night sky to the shepherds; that Jesus really was born to a virgin, and so forth. It didn't occur to me to wonder, "Now, how much of this is historically factual, and how much is metaphorical narrative?" I simply heard these stories as true. Moreover, it took no effort to do so. In particular, it didn't require faith. I had no reason to think otherwise.

Critical thinking begins in late childhood and early adolescence. One doesn't have to be an intellectual or go to college for this to happen; rather, it is a natural stage of human development. In this stage, consciously or quite unconsciously, we sift through what we learned as children to see how much of it we should keep. Is there really a tooth fairy? Are babies brought by storks (are children ever told that anymore)? Were Adam and Eve real people? In modern western culture, as noted earlier, critical thinking is very much concerned with factuality, and is thus deeply corrosive of religion in general and Christianity and the Bible in particular. In this state, we no longer hear the biblical stories as true stories or, at the least, their truth has become suspect: now it takes faith to believe them. And faith becomes believing things that you would otherwise reject.

Post-critical naïveté is the ability to hear the biblical stories once again as true stories, even as you know that they may not be factually true, and that their truth does not depend upon their factuality. My favorite way of illustrating this state is with words used by a native American story-teller. Each time he tells his tribe's story of creation, he begins, "Now I don't know if it happened this way or not, but I know this story is true." If you can get your mind around that statement, then you know what post-critical naïveté is.

Importantly, post-critical naïveté is not a return to pre-critical naïveté. It brings critical awareness with it, even as it integrates that awareness into a larger whole. It is the ability to hear the Christmas stories once again as true stories, even though you know that the story of the star and the wisemen bringing gifts is most likely Matthew's literary creation based on Isaiah 60, that Jesus was most likely born in Nazareth and not Bethlehem, that there was no massacre of the infants, and so forth. For now the truth of the stories lies in their meanings as metaphorical narratives that speak about the divine-human relationship.

Though the movement from pre-critical naïveté into critical thinking is inevitable, there is nothing inevitable about moving into the state of post-critical naïveté. One can remain in the state of critical thinking all of one's life. Though the initial movement into critical thinking can be experienced as liberating, if one remains in this state for decade after decade, it can become a very arid and barren place, like T. S. Eliot's "wasteland." We need to be led into the state of post-critical naïveté, and this is one of the major tasks in our time for Christian educators, clergy and laity alike.

5. Seeing the Bible as lens and sacrament. For my last point, I use a double metaphor: Bible as "lens" and "sacrament." I move into the point by contrasting this way of seeing with two other ways of seeing the Bible. The first affirms that the Bible is a divine product, and that's why it matters. The second affirms that the Bible is a human product, and draws the inference that it is therefore nothing special. This is what many of our fundamentalist and conservative Christian brothers and sisters fear — that if one let's go of the notion that the Bible is a divine product, it becomes just another ancient text of no particular importance.

The third option — the Bible as lens and sacrament — is the one with which I will conclude. I illustrate this option with a story. Each year at Oregon State I teach an introductory level course on the Bible. From teaching the course for two decades, I know that about twenty per cent of the students who sign up for it will be conservative Christians. Either they grew up in a conservative Christian church and family, or they are recent converts to a conservative form of college Christianity such as Campus Crusade for Christ or Navigators or Intervarsity Fellowship.

Because I know this, I use the whole of the first class period to explain as clearly as I can the perspective or vantage point from which the course will be taught. I tell my class that the perspective is the academic discipline of biblical scholarship. I tell them about the origins of the discipline some three centuries ago, dip into its history for exciting and illuminating episodes, and emphasize that it sees the Bible as a human cultural product, not as a divine product (as I did earlier in this lecture).

Furthermore, I tell them that I am emphasizing this the first day so that, if this doesn't sound like their cup of tea, they can drop the course and sign up for another course before it's too late. I also tell them that I'm not trying to get rid of them, and that I hope they will stay. To their credit, they almost always do stay. But in spite of all this careful explanation, the first few weeks of each term typically involve a lot of squabbling between me and the more bold and articulate conservative students. I don't mind, and the conflict is most often pedagogically useful.

One year I happened to have a Muslim engineering student in the class. A Muslim from the Middle East and not from North America, he signed up for it because he needed one more humanities course in order to graduate, and this one met at the right time. About two weeks into the term, after listening to the continuing conflict between me and some of the conservative students, he came up to me after class and said, "I think I'm beginning to understand what's going on here. You're saying that the Bible is like a lens through which we see God; and they're saying that it's important to believe in the lens." I looked at him and said, "Yeah, that's what I'm saying."

The distinction between "seeing the Bible as a lens" and "believing in the lens" is crucial for the re-visioning I am suggesting. Ever since much of the Bible began to be called into question by Enlightenment modes of thought, many Christians have thought that being a Christian meant "believing in the lens" in spite of rational reasons for not doing so. Christian faith began to mean "believing in the Christian tradition." The lens became the object of belief rather than a way of seeing.

But ultimately the lens metaphor is inadequate and I need to supplement it with a second metaphor: the Bible as sacrament. Within the discipline of religious studies, a sacrament is a mediator of the sacred, a means by which God becomes present to us. The point is not to believe in the sacrament, but to let it do its work. As I see it, the Bible is not simply a lens through which we see God, but also a sacrament — a means whereby the Spirit of God continues to speak to us to this day. This is most obvious in the private contemplative and devotional use of the Bible, but it can also happen in the public use of the Bible in Christian worship and preaching.

Seeing the Bible as sacrament also enables us to understand what it means to say that the Bible is "the Word of God." The older conventional way of seeing the Bible understood "Word of God" to mean that the Bible is a divine product. But I find it significant that the Christian tradition does not speak of the Bible as "the words of God" (lower case "w" and plural), but as "the Word of God" (capital "w" and singular). The former would suggest that the Bible is a divine product. But the latter suggests that the word "Word" is being used in a special sense, indeed that it is being used metaphorically. A word is a means of communication, a means of disclosing oneself, a bridge. To speak of the Bible as "the Word of God" is thus to affirm that it is a means whereby the Spirit continues to speak to us to this day. In short, as sacrament, the Bible is "Word of God" in its function, not in its origin.

Conclusion

Thus the re-visioning I am suggesting points to a sacramental way of seeing the Bible and the Christian tradition. It leads to a relational understanding of the Christian life: at its center is a relationship with God as mediated by the Christian tradition as sacrament.

This sacramental and relational vision of the Christian life is very ancient as well as quite different from the emphasis on "believing" that has marked much of modern western Christianity. But it seems to me that being a Christian is not about "believing in Christianity." One can believe all the right things and still be a jerk, or in bondage, or miserable.

We are not meant to believe in the Christian tradition, but to live within it. Being a Christian is about living within this tradition, especially the Bible as its foundation, and letting it function as both lens and sacrament, a mediator of the sacred, a means whereby God speaks to us even now.

This way of seeing Christianity also affects how we see the question of truth. The question no longer is, "Are all the stories of the Bible and the claims of the tradition factually true?" Rather, the question becomes, "Is the Christian tradition a sacrament of the sacred?" Everything I know — about religions in general, and about

Christianity, and about experience — leads me to answer with a resounding and unambiguous "Yes." When Christianity lets go of its claim to be the only true religion and accepts its status as one of the world's great religions, it has enormous credibility — not as a set of statements to be believed, but as a sacrament of the sacred.

Thus being Christian is about living within this tradition and letting it — its Scriptures, its practices, its worship — perform its sacramental function of transforming us. Ultimately, it seems to me, this understanding is both very simple and very orthodox.

Notes

1. For a fuller treatment of the material treated in this section, see my *The God We Never Knew* (San Francisco: Harper, 1997), chaps. 1–3.
2. See especially *Jesus: A New Vision* (1987), *Meeting Jesus Again for the First Time* (1994), and (with N. T. Wright) *The Meaning of Jesus: Two Visions* (1998), all published by Harper San Francisco.
3. Albert Nolan, *Jesus Before Christianity* (Maryknoll: Orbis, 1978), p. 117.

John Shelby Spong

Christ and the Body of Christ

What Will the Church of Tomorrow Be?

Recently I published a book entitled *Why Christianity Must Change or Die: A Bishop Speaks to Believers in Exile.* Simultaneously with that publication, in Luther-like fashion, I posted on the Internet Twelve Theses drawn from this book that I believe must be engaged and debated by Christians if we want Christianity to continue to live (see Appendix). In both the book and the theses I was seeking to raise to consciousness the fact that the primary myth around which traditional Christianity has organized itself has become inoperative. The supernatural, external deity who lives somewhere beyond the sky, watching over this planet, keeping a record book on the basis of which the final judgment will occur and periodically invading the world to accomplish the divine will, has become, quite frankly, unbelievable. This theistic God is today the victim of an expanded human knowledge which has emerged in the western world over the last 400 years.

That, I hope you recognize, is not a minor statement for a bishop of the church to make, for this theistic God is the deity most clearly described in the sacred scriptures of the Judeo-Christian tradition, and this is the deity most often worshipped and prayed to by Christian people. For a bishop to suggest that this deity has become an unbelievable God is to say something that to many Christians is both radical and fearful, perhaps even scandalous. In the biblical story it is obviously a theistic deity who walks with Adam and Eve in the Garden of Eden, who banishes the primeval couple after they have broken the divine prohibition and have eaten the fruit of the tree of knowledge of good and evil, and who places an angel with a drawn sword at the entrance to this garden so that they can never return. People argue that these divine acts are not history, but part of a Hebrew myth. That is true enough. But as the biblical story continues and legend, mythology and history are woven together, the God concept that informs each new episode remains that of a supernatural human being — a theistic God.

We see this invasive, personal, theistic God in the call of Abraham, in the choice of Isaac's wife, in the election of Jacob over Esau and in the favor bestowed on Joseph beyond that which was accorded to his brothers. It is a theistic God who calls Moses to deliver the people of Israel from bondage in Egypt, who equips Moses with magical powers, who visits plague after plague upon the Egyptian people, and who finally murders the firstborn of every Egyptian household in an act of divine yet immoral fury.

It is the theistic God who splits the Red Sea, rains heavenly bread called "manna" upon the chosen people in the wilderness, fights the enemies of Israel and dictates the divine rules to govern human behavior on Mt. Sinai. If this theistic definition of God is no longer believable, as I am suggesting, then we need to face the fact that the God most frequently portrayed in our own biblical story has become inoperative. Hence we are dealing with a significant crisis of faith.

Many forces have conspired to destroy this theistic deity. Theism was wounded when human beings began to embrace the vastness of the universe. Theism became all but irrelevant when the laws of cause and effect that seem to govern the natural order were discovered. Theism's mortality became apparent when such things as the weather and the causes of sicknesses were secularized and when that secular mentality then created such curative agents as antibiotics, surgery and chemotherapy all of which were morally neutral, working as effectively on sinners as they did on saints. When the weather was understood not as the result of God's wrath, but as the result of such things as El Niño winds and low pressure systems, or when the victory or defeat of a nation in military conflict was explained not on the basis of divine intervention, but rather on which nation had the larger army and the greater military capability, the theistic God was clearly fading from view. So many of the things that we once attributed to this theistic deity we now explain with no mention of supernatural power at all. Indeed, English theologian Michael Donald Goulder, New Testament Professor at The University of Birmingham, explaining his withdrawal from the Christian church, said that the theistic God of traditional Christianity no longer had any real work to do. He was unwilling to worship what he called an "unemployed deity."

To draw the potential trauma of the demise of theism even more tightly, we Christians need to face the fact that the heart of our faith story rests on the assumption that it is this theistic God who has been met incarnate in Jesus the Christ. The interpretive framework which Christians have traditionally wrapped around this Jesus is based upon the assumption that in the Christ figure the theistic God from beyond the sky has entered human history and has been encountered in human form. The first generation of Christians dealt with the logical problems of relating the external God to the human Jesus by providing this theistic deity with a landing field, a point of entry into human life. We call it the Virgin Birth. Next they described this divinely conceived one as capable of wrestling with and defeating the demonic forces that tempted him, produced mental illnesses and bound human lives in various states of ill health. They attributed to this Jesus the power they believed resided in the theistic God. Like God, Jesus was said to be able to command the natural forces of the universe. He could still the storm, calming both wind and wave, he could walk on water, he could expand the food supply so dramatically that five loaves of bread could feed 5000 people. He was also capable of performing other miracles. He could give sight to the blind and hearing to the deaf. Like God, Jesus could forgive sins and promise paradise. Even death faded before him. He could raise the four-days-dead Lazarus and walk physically out of his own tomb, aided by angelic beings who came from heaven to roll away the stone. Finally, when his work was complete, he was said to return to the place the theistic God was thought to live. He needed a round-trip ticket and thus a proper exit from this world. So in a gravity-defying act, it was said that Jesus ascended into the sky to be reunited with the theistic supernatural deity. Contemporary biblical theologians today seek to explain these stories in a wide variety of ways, but the fact remains that all of them reflect a definition of God that is theistic. God is a Being supernatural in power, dwelling outside this world and periodically invading history in miraculous ways.

If this theistic, supernatural understanding of God has in our time ceased to be a believable concept as I have suggested, then we Christians must also face the fact that so has this traditional interpretation of Jesus as the incarnation of this theistic deity. Yet that definition remains the primary understanding of Jesus upon which the Christian Church is still organized and that is the primary basis upon which the Church continues to claim its power at this moment. Significant portions of that church assert, for example, that only through the official sacraments can the grace of this theistic God be mediated to human life. The authority of the church's clergy is still primarily located in their ability to preside over those sacraments. Clergy power is still vested in the claim, made in both Protestant and Catholic traditions, that in some sense the ordained one stands between the supernatural deity and the frightened and insecure human beings, who are defined as fallen, fragile sinners unable to save themselves. The Church, the sacraments, the clergy are the mediators of salvation that comes from above.

Almost all of our physical church structures reflect this theistic understanding of God. Flying buttresses, Gothic arches, massive steeples and pointed windows, are designed to direct the worshippers to the God who dwells above the sky. When one adds to those structures the stained-glass windows which seek to capture the biblical scenes in a kind of eternal timelessness, one understands that churches were traditionally built to proclaim in stone and wood that the ultimate meaning of human life is found beyond life where the theistic God reigns. This theistic understanding was a compact, snug and comfortable statement of who God is, what the universe is and what our place within it is. But it is this very world view that has now been obliterated.

Galileo, building on the work of Copernicus and Kepler, has made us aware that the three-tiered view of the universe, assumed in our theistic definition of God, no longer exists. Our tiny planet Earth circles around a mid-sized star called the Sun, which is part of a galaxy of one billion stars in a universe that contains at least 125 billion other galaxies. The theistic God above our sky is no more. Before that realization had been absorbed, Isaac Newton began to squeeze the presence of miracle and magic out of life, reducing dramatically the arenas in which the theistic God was believed to be able to operate.

Next, Charles Darwin challenged the myth of our special creation in God's image. He also raised questions about the human self-definition gleaned from the biblical story that we are those who, though created perfect, had fallen into sin so total and so complete that only the theistic God could rescue us. Darwin provided us with a countering image. Human beings, he suggested, like all other forms of life, have emerged out of the evolutionary struggle to survive. They were never created perfect so they could not have fallen. If this Darwinian view is correct, as I think it is, then it immediately invalidates the traditional understanding of the saving work of Christ as the one who was the theistic God's emissary to rescue the fallen sinner, the one who accomplished atonement by means of his sacrificial death which somehow paid the necessary price required for our restitution. That understanding of the saving work of the Christ still undergirds traditional Christian liturgies and still provides the content of many of our familiar hymns. But those images have become inoperative in a post-Darwinian world. For if we are not fallen, sinful, helpless creatures as the Bible has proclaimed, but are rather unfinished, still evolving, emerging creatures as Darwin has suggested, it is not rescue but empowerment to take the next step into an ever-deepening humanity that we require.

Next, Sigmund Freud forced us to look at the infantile and oedipal aspects present in our traditional faith story. Then Albert Einstein confronted us with the reality of relativity, not just in the world of time and space, but in the religious claims we make for both God and Christ, as well as in the authoritative claims with which we have surrounded our creeds and doctrines. The security found in the Christian assertion that we are in possession of Divine Truth revealed directly by this theistic God in either scripture or tradition has been obliterated. In turn, this has rendered such Christian assertions as papal infallibility and biblical inerrancy to be no more than an ecclesiastical version of the Maginot Line behind which deluded people hide with false expectations.

That, in thumbnail brevity, is why I have asserted that Christianity must change or die. This faith tradition can no longer rest on the fading theistic claims of yesterday. The presuppositions upon which Christianity was built are not today sustainable. If Christianity is to survive, it will require a radical, new reformation that will recast every aspect of this ancient faith story. That is also why I have suggested that the reformation that is now upon the Christian Church will make the reformation of the 16th century seem, by comparison, to be something like a Sunday school tea party.

I have no joy, no glee and no sense of triumph in stating these things to my Christian brothers and sisters. I do it because I regard these things as the difficult but unavoidable realities that I as a Christian must face. I am not an enemy of Christianity in its essence. I am rather a deeply committed Christian believer. With all my being, I still acknowledge that Jesus of Nazareth is for me the meeting place between God and human life. I call this Jesus the Christ. I acknowledge him as Lord of my life. I am not a peripheral Christian. I have served the Christian Church as one baptized in infancy, confirmed in puberty and married before its altar. I have accompanied my father, my mother, my wife and many of my friends into that church to hear the words of the burial of the dead read over them. I intend to die as a loyal member of this worshipping tradition.

Nor do I do these things simply, as my secular friends charge, because I cannot escape the habits of a lifetime. I act out of a compelling and living faith. This church has ordained me deacon and priest and it was willing to accept my service in these roles for 21 years. This church then elected and consecrated me to be one of its bishops and I have fulfilled that responsibility for 24 years. I deeply love this church. I treasure its faith story. But I am also convinced that the heart will never worship what the mind rejects. Today the theistic understanding of God as a supernatural Being, external to life, who invades the world in miraculous ways is no longer a God that the mind can accept and therefore no longer a God that the heart can worship. Since this definition of God lies at the heart of our understanding of Christ, and the way in which the life of the Christian Church is organized, then to that degree the whole Christian enterprise is tottering. If we cannot change those presuppositions, if there is no other way to portray God, to understand the work of Christ and to organize the church, then Christianity will surely die.

If we Christians would only open our eyes to see, that death is becoming apparent everywhere we look. The Christian churches across Europe are all but extinct as places of worship. In France churches are most frequently used as museums or settings for weddings. In England churches cover the land but attract more tourists than they do members. Of England's 70,000,000 citizens only about 1,000,000 attend church with any regularity. Polls in Australia and New Zealand reveal that less than 20 percent of the population of those two countries even claim a relationship, however tenuous, with an organized religious tradition. There was a burst of renewed religious interest in Poland, Russia and Eastern Europe after the fall of Communism, but it was short lived and the real winner there, as time has demonstrated, was not Christianity but secularism. Eastern Orthodoxy is treated in those lands where it remains the dominant Christian tradition as but a benign irrelevance from another age. Only in Africa and in other parts of the Third World is there numerical Christian growth, but a careful analysis of that growth in those places reveals that it is largely of a Christianity marked by a pre-modern superstitious literalism. It is not a Christianity that will ever engage the post-modern world. That these Third World churches attempt to solve complex ethical issues by quoting the words of Scripture is not a sign of new life. The failure of this Third World fundamentalism to engage their people's ancient prejudices about women or homosexuals or even to illumine the bitterness of some of their tribal struggles relegates it to a pre-modern yesterday, not a post-modern tomorrow. This kind of Christianity will never survive the Internet-related and email-connected world into which even Africa is now awakening.

In the United States mainline churches are in a statistical free fall. That is frequently masked in parts of the south and midwest where religion is still big business, but the fact remains that Christianity loses what business leaders refer to as "market share" every year, both in the United States and in the world. Among Roman Catholics there is an enormous and growing clergy shortage and, according to many studies, the people who do pursue the priesthood in that church today are in large measure extremely conservative security seekers who will not engage modern learning except to condemn it in the name of the True Church. That is hardly a stance that will be successful.

When one listens to the guardians of the various ecclesiastical establishments as they seek to explain these statistical realities, one is amazed at the capacity for self-deception.

The current drastic decline in the power of institutional Christianity is occurring not because of liberal compromises with the ancient verities, but because the traditional basis upon which this faith system has been erected can no longer be sustained. The heart will never worship what the mind rejects. It is only when that reality is faced honestly by institutional leaders that we will finally stop tinkering around the edges of church life, as if minor adjustments here and there will restore our ship of faith to smooth sailing. That is of no more value than doing a facelift on a corpse and pretending that the corpse is still alive. When these realities are finally recognized by Church leaders, then perhaps the need for a total new reformation will become both imperative and unavoidable. The real issue before the church today is not whether Christianity in its traditional form is dying. That appears to be obvious. The real issue is whether a reformation this radical, one that raises questions about the very basis of our faith, is something that the Christian Church in its present form is strong enough to tolerate, much less to embrace. Can we as a church, for example, dismiss theism as an adequate definition of God, without slipping into an atheism which even our language suggests is the only alternative? If we can no longer explain the Christ in any terms other than as the incarnation of the theistic God, is there any way we can still affirm that basic Christian principle that God was in this Christ? If we surrender the sense of an external, supernatural deity, can we continue to pray? If there is no revealed will of this theistic deity in such things as the Ten Commandments or the Holy Scriptures, is there still a way we can talk about Christian ethics? If there is no judge keeping record books in the sky and thus no ultimate behavior-controlling sense of heaven as a place of reward or hell as a place of punishment, is there still a way in which eternal life can be affirmed? When those who were once called liberal Christians take leave of the church to join the secular city, I fear they answer these questions with a sad, but resolute, no. Fundamentalists, on the other hand, will not even raise these questions. The time has come for those of us, the ones I call believers in exile, those who can neither be fundamentalists nor abandon the faith of their fathers and mothers, to ask whether or not these are our only two alternatives.

Because I believe there is another possibility beyond these two sterile choices, I am now compelled to suggest that a sweeping total, radical reformation is the only option the Christian Church has if it wishes to avoid institutional death. Contrary to the reformation of the sixteenth century which was primarily about authority, valid ministry and who had the power on this earth to represent God, this new reformation must be radically theological for it must address the assumptions at the heart of the Christian claim.

There will be many other differences between this reformation that stands before the Christian world today and the movement that coined that word at the time of Luther, Calvin, Zwingli and Cranmer. This reformation will not come from within a powerful ecclesiastical institution that is abusing its privileged position. It must come out of a weakened and dying institution that society has already marginalized. It will occur in a world where theology is thought of as esoteric and in which politicians will yawn before they will go to war over theological issues. It will come at a time when for countless numbers of people the word "God" no longer stands for a power to be feared or a reality to be courted. It will come at a time when the meaning of human life is being reassessed under the challenges of modern science. It will come at a time when the literalness of the theological framework with which we have surrounded the Christ figure is being challenged by our own Christian scholarship. It will come at a time when the words we have traditionally used to describe the atoning death and saving work of Jesus have become in quick succession first strange, then bizarre and finally repelling. Our world will never be drawn to a religion which suggests that salvation comes through a human sacrifice of one who was crucified to appease an offended theistic deity. Neither will it be attracted to the idea that in the shedding of Jesus' blood somehow the price of sin was paid. These threadbare concepts are not worthy today of eliciting worship. Indeed, they have actually become grotesque. The next reformation will have to be born inside a Christianity that is visibly staggering and deeply divided.

Some Christians, I fear, will continue their efforts to meet this crisis by shouting their ancient creeds and quoting their ancient scriptures with increasing fervor, as if these words had actually captured God and God's unchanging truth. These will, of course, be the conservative evangelicals or the neo-fundamentalists. As the expansion of knowledge moves inexorably forward, their approach will look increasingly neurotic and it will appeal primarily to the spiritually uninformed and the immature. It will also succeed only in building a religious ghetto mentality.

There will also be other Christians who, rejecting that fundamentalist alternative, will express a willingness to surrender their literalized faith story bit by bit as new knowledge seems to require, hoping that by sacrificing peripheral things they can protect essential things. These people are, of course, the moderates or the liberals. But their approach will succeed only in slowing down the death process. They will not alter the eventual outcome. The fundamentalists will finally go down in flames while the liberals will expire with a pitiful whimper. Either way, the result will be the same. Death appears to be Christianity's destiny unless something radically different invades this tradition.

When both the fundamentalist and liberal approaches are seen to be dead-ends, then the final alternative will emerge as a distinct choice which just might enable Christianity to have a new birth in the new millennium. That choice begins with the recognition of the theological fact that the experience of God is never to be identified with explanations of that experience, no matter how sacred a part of our tradition the explanations have become. The Gospels, for example, are first century, predominantly Jewish explanations trying to make sense out of an experience that somehow in Jesus of Nazareth the holy God had been met in a new way. But when these first century Jewish people sought to explain that experience, they did so in terms of the theistic God of the Exodus, Mt. Sinai, the Promised Land and the Exile. The Gospels point to the God experience that was in Christ. The interpretive explanations found in the Gospels cannot be identified with the God experience itself. The Gospels are not magic. The Gospels are not inerrant. No human explanation can finally claim that. The Gospels, along with the rest of the Bible, are not in any literal sense "the words of God."

The historic creeds of the church are also explanations. They were shaped by the Mediterranean Greek-thinking minds of the fourth and fifth centuries of the Christian Era. Inside this frame of reference they sought to make sense of how God was experienced in the created world, in Jesus and in the spirit-filled life of the Church. The doctrine of the Holy Trinity was their attempt to explain their experience. The creeds do not capture that God experience. No explanation can do that. The creeds only try to make sense out of it. Creeds are not themselves sacred, infallible, or unchanging. The best creeds can do is to point to truth. They cannot be identified with truth. So creeds, like all explanations, will not endure forever.

There are no words, no traditions, and no theological formulas that are not explanations, and every explanation is time-limited, and its "truth" is time-bound. Theism, we need to understand, is but another explanation of a God experience. The death of an explanation does not require the denial of the experience. So all of these symbols of our faith story — our Bible, our creeds, our doctrines, our sacred traditions — can be and must be debated, compromised, changed and even surrendered if necessary. Only the experience of God is eternal and that experience ultimately has no words. The words we apply to that experience must be broken open in every generation, because when words are added to experience, the eternal quality of the experience is immediately distorted. The experience of God cannot, therefore, finally be reduced to either scripture or creeds. Not understanding that, the church has attempted to make idols of both. Today those idols are dying and they must be transcended if we are to find a pathway into a living future.

So the reformation which the church must inaugurate today must be allowed to raise even life and death questions about every Christian claim. It must be allowed to challenge every Christian formulation. It must explore the experience of God beyond the definition of theism. It must look at the meaning of Jesus apart from the theological doctrines of Incarnation and Atonement. It must examine human life as an emerging, evolutionary being, not as a fallen, once-perfect creation. It must sacrifice the pre-modern claims of miracle and magic, surrender the concept of a supernatural, invasive deity and abandon the mythological framework that portrayed Jesus as a visiting, saving, divine figure.

Can these questions be raised by those of us who are still believers? Will those who argue for a God understood as something other than the supernatural supreme being of classical theism, or for a Jesus whose full humanity becomes the means through which the Ground of All Being is revealed, or for a concept of spirit that issues not in piety, but in human wholeness, still be seen as the descendants of classical Christianity? Can a church that makes no claim to mediate an external God to an earth-bound population through its scriptures, creeds and sacramental acts ever see itself as the next step in the evolution of Christianity?

I stand before the world today as one who believes that the answer to each of these queries is yes. That is why I continue to be a Christian. God is real for me, a mystical, undefinable presence that I can experience but never explain. I experience God as the source of life in the act of living fully. I experience God as the source of love in the act of loving wastefully. I experience God as the Ground of Being in the act of having the courage to be. Jesus is the revelation of this God for me, not because of miracle stories or excessive pre-modern claims, but because he is portrayed as one who is fully alive with the life of God, totally loving with the love of God, and as one who possesses the capacity to be all that he could be revealing the very Ground of Being that I call God. I serve the God that I meet in Jesus, not by trying to convert others to my way of believing, but by seeking to transform the world so that every person might have that God-like capacity to live fully, to love wastefully and to be all that each person can be.

Finally, I yearn to be part of a newly understood Christian Church, one that is not dedicated to the maintenance of its institutional power, but rather one that will both assist people into life and one that will lobby in word and deed for the removal of any barriers that impede anyone's humanity. I want to be part of a Christian fellowship that will not only help me to appropriate the religious heritage of my own tradition but will also allow me to receive the spiritual insights emerging out of faith traditions different from my own. I want to sit in a worship setting where I will hear sermons that will assist me to find meaning in my life, engage in liturgies that will open me to all that is and allow me to explore even the dimensions of life hidden in my unconscious self. I want to be part of a Church whose clergy are well trained, but whose authority will be in their ability to teach and to explore the nature of truth, not in the status of their presumed ordained role as the mediators of the divine. I want to be part of a community that can make me aware of the reality in which I live and move and have my being. I want to call that reality God without having that word distort the meaning I seek to express by relating that word to all of the God concepts of antiquity.

I already see the signs of this reformation appearing ever so tentatively in the life of the Christian Church. It is present in the inclusion of women, in the new and growing consciousness about sexual orientation, in the experimentation taking place in liturgy, in the altars that have been moved from the back walls of the churches so the priest can now face not the God out there, but the God present in the midst of the people they serve, and in the radical and increasingly popular stances of frontier Christian thinkers who call us beyond yesterday's boundaries. Those younger than I will live to see the growing power of this radical reformation. It is a reformation that must not be stopped, for to stop it is to watch Christianity die the death of irrelevance. I am moreover convinced it cannot be stopped, for it seeks to explore something that is both real and compelling. So let the reformation begin!

I will rejoice if I am remembered as one who, in some small way, encouraged its birth.

Appendix

Twelve Theses

1. Theism, as a way of defining God is dead. God can no longer be understood with credibility as a Being supernatural in power, dwelling above the sky and prepared to invade human history periodically to enforce the divine will. So, most theological God-talk is today meaningless unless we find a new way to speak of God.

2. Since God can no longer be conceived in theistic terms, it becomes nonsensical to seek to understand Jesus as the incarnation of the theistic deity. So, the Christology of the ages is bankrupt.

3. The biblical story of the perfect and finished creation from which human beings fell into sin is pre-Darwinian mythology and post-Darwinian nonsense.
4. The virgin birth, understood as literal biology, makes the divinity of Christ, as traditionally understood, impossible.
5. The miracle stories of the New Testament can no longer be interpreted in a post-Newtonian world as supernatural events performed by an incarnate deity.
6. The view of the cross as the sacrifice for the sins of the world is a barbaric idea based on primitive concepts of God that must be dismissed.
7. Resurrection is an action of God, who raised Jesus into the meaning of God. It therefore cannot be a physical resuscitation occurring inside human history.
8. The story of the ascension assumed a three-tiered universe and is therefore not capable of being translated into the concepts of a post-Copernican space age.
9. There is no external, objective, revealed standard writ in scripture or on tablets of stone that will govern our ethical behavior for all time.
10. Prayer cannot be a request made to a theistic deity to act in human history in a particular way.
11. The hope for life after death must be separated forever from the behavior control mentality of reward and punishment. The Church must abandon, therefore, its reliance on guilt as a motivator of behavior.
12. All human beings bear God's image and must be respected for what each person is. Therefore, no external description of one's being, whether based on race, ethnicity, gender or sexual orientation, can properly be used as the basis for either rejection or discrimination.

*Drawn from the book *Why Christianity Must Change or Die* by John Shelby Spong.

Karen L. King

Back to the Future
Jesus and Heresy

Twentieth-century Bookends: Adolph von Harnack and the Jesus Seminar

I t might seem as though little has changed in the last century. After all, about a hundred years ago, the radical German Protestant historian and theologian Adolf von Harnack had already located the essence of Jesus' message in his parables and in his teaching of the kingdom. "If anyone wants to know what the kingdom of God and the coming of it meant in Jesus' message," Harnack wrote, that person "must read and study his parables."[1] When people do, what they find, says Harnack, is that Jesus' message was not concerned with apocalyptic eschatology, with "external hopes for the future."[2] The message of Jesus was and still is, he says, about the relation of the soul to God. As Harnack puts it: " . . . that the kingdom of God 'cometh not with observation,' that it is already here, was [Jesus'] own vision."[3] Harnack came to this position by sifting through the available data, distinguishing "what is traditional and what is peculiar," that is, what he regarded as traditional to Judaism or Hellenism from what he found to be peculiar to Jesus's teaching.[4]

In the end, he summarized the essence of Christianity — in a single sentence! — by saying, "The Christian religion is something simple and sublime; it means one thing and one thing only: Eternal life in the midst of time, by the strength and under the eyes of God."[5] This life, Harnack stated, was fully expressed in the teachings of Jesus, which he summarized in a rather parsimonious form as:

> Firstly the kingdom of God and its coming.
> Secondly, God the Father and the infinite value of the human soul.

77

Thirdly, the higher righteousness and the commandment of love.[6]

Although framed rhetorically in contrast to Judaism and Catholicism, Harnack's appeal to Jesus and his teaching was aimed primarily against what he took to be the rigidification of his beloved Protestantism into an authoritarian and defensive orthodoxy in his own day. He lamented changes in Christianity in which:

> The living faith seems to be transformed into a creed to be believed; devotion to Christ, into Christology; the ardent hope for the coming of 'the kingdom,' into a doctrine of immortality and deification; prophecy into technical exegesis and theological learning; the ministers of the Spirit, into clerics; the brothers [and sisters] into lay[people] in a state of tutelage; miracles and miraculous cures disappear altogether or are priestly devices; fervent prayers become solemn hymns and litanies; the 'Spirit' becomes law and compulsion.[7]

There would seem to be a lot of similarity in Harnack both to the process and results of the Jesus Seminar. We, too, began with the parables.[8] We have placed Jesus' teaching of the kingdom at the core of our data base of authentic Jesus material. We have argued that the apocalyptic eschatology in the Gospel traditions for the most part does not belong to the earliest layer of the tradition, to that layer which one might ascribe to Jesus himself. We have done that by carefully sifting piece by piece through the available data, distinguishing what is distinctive about Jesus from materials common to the general cultural milieu or arguably belonging to later church concerns. And to varying degrees, with varying emphases, many of the scholars of the Jesus Seminar also understand this work as a wedge against the ways in which the figure of Jesus is used and misused to further anti-intellectual, authoritarian, and rigidifying aims in our own day.

So, too, the critics of Harnack and the critics of the Jesus Seminar would seem to be making quite similar complaints along similar lines. Harnack was severely criticized for rending too great a gap between the teachings of Jesus and the Christ of the gospels, and for severing the essential relationship between Jesus and Judaism. So, too, critics of the Jesus Seminar have sounded similar notes, insisting that we have gone too far, that our results open up a gulf between Jesus and traditional Christian statements of belief that destroys the possibility of faith and the life of the Church. We draw a cynical black line, they say, crossing out gospel messages that believers have found to carry the basis of their faith and hope, and drawing in red a Jesus more amenable to our tastes. They say, too, that because we argue that Jesus' teaching was not centrally concerned with the future coming of the kingdom, was not expressed primarily in terms of apocalyptic-mythic language, that we have invented a non-Jewish Jesus. A further look at these criticisms and what is at stake is warranted.

In 1904, the French Catholic modernist, Alfred Loisy, took Harnack to task quite severely in *L'Evangile et l'eglise*.[9] He took umbrage with the very suggestion that Christ[10] and his gospel could be properly understood apart from the tradition of the Church:

> Whatever one thinks theologically, of tradition, whether we trust it or regard it with suspicion, we know Christ only by the tradition, across the tradition, and in the tradition of the primitive Christians. This is as much to say that Christ is inseparable from His work, and that the attempt to define the essence of Christianity according to the pure gospel of Jesus, apart from tradition, cannot succeed.[11]

But Loisy's point was not merely that Christ is impossible to locate apart from church tradition, but that there is, in his opinion, no need to make such a distinction at all. For him there is no difference in essence between Christ and Christianity:

> The historian will find that the essence of Christianity has been more or less preserved in the different Christian communities; [s/]he will not expect this essence to have been absolutely and definitely realized at any point of past centuries; [s/]he will believe that it has been realized more or less perfectly from the beginning, and that it will continue to be realized thus more and more, so long as Christianity shall endure.[12]

Precisely because he doesn't distinguish between them, the separation Harnack makes between Jesus and the later Church appears to Loisy not only artificial, but distorting. As Robert Funk has repeatedly pointed out in the Seminar, the basic issue at stake in this debate concerns where the Christian revelation is understood to be located: in the distinctive teaching of Jesus (as Harnack) or in the tradition of the Church (as Loisy).[13]

Loisy also objected vociferously to separating the essence, if not the form, of Jesus' teachings from Judaism: "It is . . . in the highest degree arbitrary," he wrote, "to decide that Christianity in its essence just be all that the gospel has not borrowed from Judaism, as if all that the gospel has retained of the Jewish tradition must necessarily be of secondary value."[14] This objection did not arise because Loisy had a more positive or more accurate view of Judaism than that of Harnack. Harnack had indeed disparaged Judaism, caricaturing it as a legalistic, particularistic tradition, mired in a mythology from which Christianity had to escape in order to fulfill its destiny as "a universal spiritual power."[15] Loisy, too, understood Christianity as superior to the Judaism of the Old Testament, but he stressed the continuity between the two: "If His [Christ's] way of understanding and realizing God, Love and the kingdom, is more pure, more deep, more living than that of the Old Testament, it perfects what has preceded it and does not destroy it."[16] Similarly, he argues that while the idea of the reign of God was present in Judaism before Jesus, his teaching is superior: "In the gospel, the national element has disappeared, the nationality of Israelite being no longer in itself a title to the kingdom; the eschatological element no longer fills the view, and the religious and moral element comes into the foreground."[17] The primary difference between Christianity and Judaism for Loisy lay only "in that 'fulfilment' which is the special feature of the gospel."[18] His disagreement with Harnack, therefore, was not about Harnack's characterization of Judaism as inferior to Christianity, but rather about his theology. For Loisy, the intimate connection between Christianity and Judaism could not be severed without sacrificing the traditional supersessionist theological position that Christianity was the fulfillment of Judaism.[19]

The German New Testament scholar and theologian, Rudolf Bultmann, agreed with Harnack and Loisy that the specifically Jewish character of Jesus' teaching on the kingdom lay primarily in its mythic eschatology and particularistic nationalism. He also agreed with Loisy that it would be impossible to sever Jesus from his historical context. Despite the fact that Harnack had listed "the kingdom of God *and its coming*" as a central feature of the teachings of Jesus, Bultmann criticized Harnack sharply for the ease with which he dispensed with eschatology as a central feature of Jesus' teaching.[20] "There can be no doubt," he argued, "that Jesus like his contemporaries expected a tremendous eschatological drama," including the expectation of a heavenly messiah, the resurrection of the dead, and final judgement.[21] Unlike Loisy, however, Bultmann based his conviction on the Protestant historical-critical investigations of Johannes Weiss and Albert Schweitzer,[22] who had, in Bultmann's opinion, firmly established "the eschatological character of the appearance of Jesus and of his preaching of the imminent advent of the Kingdom of God."[23]

But like Loisy, Bultmann's objections to Harnack severing Jesus' teachings from Jewish eschatology were also crucial to his theology. He had built his own existential theology around the conviction that Jesus' eschatology conveyed a radical call to decision, a call whose answer "Yea, Lord" would alone make possible authentic existence before God. For Bultmann, this meant two things: First of all, he was able to argue that there was no discernable gap between the teaching of Jesus and that of the early churches, including Paul. Second, he interpreted the universality of Jesus' message quite in opposition to Harnack. For Harnack that universality was core; Bultmann insisted, however, that Jesus meant only that "the Kingdom of God was to come for the bene-fit of the Jewish people."[24] But he interprets this statement to mean that "all humanistic individualism is rejected" and "all individualistic culti-vation of the spirit, all mysticism, is excluded. Jesus calls to decision, not to inner life," thereby redirecting Harnack's vision of authentic exis-tence from an inner life linked to the living God to a vision of authentic existence as decision.[25]

Yet, in seeming contradiction, at the same time that Bultmann insists that Jesus "expected a tremendous eschatological drama," he also simultaneously insisted that Jesus "neither depicts the punishments of hell nor paints elaborate pictures of the heavenly glory. . . . Jesus thus *rejects the whole content of apocalyptic speculation*, as he rejects also the calculation of the time and the watching for signs."[26] Rather:

> The real significance of 'the Kingdom of God' for the message of Jesus does not in any sense depend on the dramatic events attending its coming, nor on any circumstances which the imag-ination can conceive. It interests him not at all as a describable state of existence, but rather as the transcendent event, which signifies for man [sic] the ultimate Either-Or, which constrains him to decision.[27] Rather, the Kingdom of God is a power *which, although it is entirely future, wholly determines the present.*[28]

It would seem that whether understood as the outer husk or as the mythological expression, both Harnack and Bultmann ultimately understand the essential meaning of Jesus' teaching about the Kingdom to concern the present, not a mythological future.

In the end, it may be that they were simply not addressing the same problem, and hence their answers differed. For Harnack, the central issue was grasping the stable and eternally valid meaning of Christianity despite the varied forms and meanings historical Christianity had taken over nearly two millennia. The goal was a vision of the unchanging in the pluriform and constantly changing life of Christianity viewed historically. For Bultmann, the central issue was bridging the gap between the worldview of antiquity and that of his own twentieth century. As Bultmann puts it:

> The problem is simply this: how is a Christian existence possible in this world when one, in both his [sic] work and pleasures, shares in its culture, its tasks, and its worldly goods? . . . Can the paradoxical situation of primitive Christianity hovering 'between the times' — that is between the 'old' and the 'new aeon' — be at all viewed as valid after the eschatalogical [sic] expectations of the first Christian generations were extinguished? Is Christian life, perceived and prescribed in the New Testament as a 'transcendental' life, viable?[29]

Bultmann is right that these were not problems that greatly troubled Harnack. Harnack takes up this topic in response to critics, whom he says claim:

> The Gospel, it is said, is a great and sublime thing and it has certainly been a saving power in history, but it is indissolubly connected with an antiquated view of the world and history; and, therefore, although it be painful to say so, and we have nothing better to put in its place, it has lost its validity and can have no further significance for us.

To this Harnack responds:

> I have tried to show what the essential elements in the Gospel are, and these elements are "timeless." Not only are they so; but the man [sic] to whom the Gospel addresses itself is also "timeless," that is to say, it is the man [sic] who, in spite of all progress and development, never changes in his [sic] inmost constitution and in his [sic] fundamental relations with the external

world. Since that is so, this Gospel remains in force, then, for us too.[30]

Here the stability of "human nature," as well as of the Gospel, makes possible a continued significance, indeed the same significance, to the Gospel across two millennia from antiquity to the twentieth century.[31]

In the end, Bultmann is concerned primarily with how the ancient Gospel can have meaning in the twentieth century; Harnack is concerned with the stability of that meaning in the face of documented changes in Christianity across its 1900-year history. Both Harnack and Bultmann see the ultimate meaning of Jesus' teaching of the kingdom as transcendent and focused upon the determination of the present relationship of God and humanity. For Bultmann, the eschatological language of the kingdom is that which brings one to decision, and hence to the possibility of authentic existence. For Harnack, the language of the kingdom and its coming express the gift of "an inner link with the living God."[32] For neither does a literal reading of Jewish apocalyptic eschatology provide the essential Christian message; indeed both share the same disparaging views of that ancient mythic worldview as primitive and unacceptable to the modern Christian life. If there is a difference in their historical reconstructions, it lies not in their views of Judaism, but only in that whereas Harnack solves "the problem" of Jewish apocalyptic mythology by *distinguishing* it from Jesus' core teaching and abstracting a transcendent essence of Christianity, Bultmann is able to solve the problem by *interpreting* that same mythology and abstracting a demythologized "transcendent kerygmatic event" from it.

The fact is that Harnack, Loisy, and Bultmann share the same Christian construction of "Judaism" and the same rather negative opinion of it, if not the same relationship of Christianity to that construct. It is questionable whether a good relationship among contemporary Jews and Christians could ever be built upon this Christian construction of Judaism, no matter how it is positioned vis-à-vis Christianity.

The Seminar addressed something of a different problem than either Harnack or Bultmann, by taking up the question of what can reliably be said historically about Jesus. This approach was raised largely by synoptic criticism and redaction-critical studies, which have made all critical scholars aware that not everything attributed to Jesus in the canonical Gospels can be attributed to him historically. Although based on earlier work and located firmly in the tradition of radical Protestant historiography,[33] Robert Funk's proposal for a collaborative and systematic attempt to evaluate the full evidence for the historical Jesus and to establish a data base for historical Jesus work was, however, new.

Yet this enterprise has become fully enmeshed in the old discourses about Christian normativity. As we have seen, in the controversy over the meaning of the data base — and who gets to say what that meaning is —, the old problems have come front and center: the relationship of Jesus to Christian teaching, and the relationship of Jesus to Judaism. Both these issues are heavily invested in discourses in which Christian claims to normativity are evaluated, and by which Christianity is defined.

The continuing centrality of these old problems and the discourses in which they are embedded are exemplified in the two most frequent criticisms of the Seminar. The first is the minimal content of the data base.[34] These results, our critics say, seem to take away too much, put too much into doubt. Conservative scholars in particular wish to defend above all the historicity of the resurrection.[35]

A second frequent criticism stems from the Seminar's results that the apocalyptic eschatology of the Gospels does not belong to the earliest layers of tradition, and hence cannot be said to stem from the historical Jesus. Here more liberal scholars enter the fray. For these critics, the rejection of Jesus as an eschatological prophet and apocalyptic teacher is directly tied to the charge that the Seminar has produced a non-Jewish Jesus.

Since the storm caused by the Jesus Seminar's claim "to liberate the non-eschatological Jesus . . . from Schweitzer's eschatological Jesus,"[36] scholars have been led to recognize that it is untenable to draw too sharp a distinction between Jewish apocalyptic and wisdom traditions. The either-or choice between a view of Jesus as eschatological prophet or wisdom sage does insufficient justice to the evidence. But muddying the waters to produce a mildly eschatological sage or a wise eschatological prophet, while perhaps with the good intent of striking a blow for civility and tolerant compromise, does not address the issues at stake, because those lie less in the results of historical reconstruction than they do in the theological consequences drawn from those reconstructions. And those consequences address nothing less than the identity of Christianity itself.

What is clear is that these criticisms of the Seminar and the discourses in which they are framed and have meaning continue to be primarily about defining and defending the normative boundaries of Christianity, not about historical methods and results. The rancorous and even venomous language of the contemporary critique bespeaks more than a loss of collegial civility; it points toward the fact that people understand what is at stake here to be the very meaning and identity of Christianity, and the debates continue to reproduce the structures, if not the precise contents, of ancient discourses of normativity.

Rather than engage these criticisms in the terms in which the debate has been laid out,[37] I would like to question the terms of the discourse itself. I have one primary point of critique: that this discourse is inadequate for dealing with issues of difference and diversity. It is inadequate to comprehend the pluriformity of Christianity, both now and throughout its global history, and it is inadequate for relating to Others, whether far distant or close neighbors.

Defining Normative Christianity

It may appear that little has changed in the twentieth century. Now at the turn to a new millennium, the debate and to a large degree even the terms of the debate have not shifted much. But the meaning of these debates has shifted a great deal, not least because the world in which we live looks so much different than it did to Harnack and Loisy. Ours is a post-Holocaust, post-colonial, post-Cold War, post-modern world. A world where most Christians no longer live in Europe and North America. A world where the site for contact among religions is no longer the purview of travelers to exotic lands, but can and does take place on the corners of any moderate-sized city in the US. It is, as Clifford Geertz puts it, a "world in pieces" in which:

> difference must be seen *not* as the negation of similarity, its opposite, its contrary and its contradiction. It must be seen as comprising it: locating it, concretizing it, giving it form. The blocs being gone, and their hegemonies with them, we are facing an era of dispersed entanglements, each distinctive. What unity there is, and what identity, is going to have to be negotiated, produced out of difference.[38]

We need to situate our questions and agendas in engagement with this world of "dissolving boundaries and vanishing borders."[39] For this we need strong theological and ethical thinking. We need, too, the approaches of religious studies, applied to our own traditions as well as those of others. For knowledge of the religious traditions of others is no longer a luxury for comparative work, but a necessity for "getting along," as they say in LA.

For these tasks, the old discourses are highly problematic. They engage in a kind of "fact fundamentalism" and a construction of the "Other" that is inimical to historical reconstruction and to a politics of justice, and therefore to sound theology. I want to look at two aspects of the ancient discourses of Christian normativity that are still operative in the historical Jesus debates. The first of these is the discourse of origins.

Writing from North Africa at the turn into the third century, the Latin presbyter Tertullian produced a book called *Prescriptions against Heretics* in which he argued that certain heresies were instigated by the devil through the influence of Greek philosophy on pure Christian faith:

> What has Jerusalem to do with Athens, the Church with the Academy, the Christian with the heretic? Our principles comes from the Porch of Solomon, who had himself taught that the Lord is to be sought in simplicity of heart. I have no use for a Stoic or a Platonic or a dialectic Christianity. After Jesus Christ we have no need of speculation, after the Gospel no need of research. When we come to believe, we have no desire to believe anything else; for we begin by believing that there is nothing else which we have to believe.[40]

Against the "human and demonic doctrines" of his opponents, Tertullian holds up a rule of faith[41] and an apostolic order[42] as the basis for truth. Such voices can still be heard in our own day whenever dogma is wielded as a weapon against critical reflection and, I would say, against the possibility of spiritual growth.

But Tertullian goes further. He roots his truth in a supposedly historical basis by arguing that: "Things of every kind must be classed according to their origin"[43] for "truth comes first and falsification afterwards."[44] "Our teaching," Tertullian writes, " is not later; it is earlier than them all. In this lies the evidence of its truth, which everywhere has the first place."[45]

In this short treatise, Tertullian sets out what became one platform in the normative treatment of difference within the history of Christianity. Origins is here linked with orthodoxy, with unity, purity, essence, and truth. Heresy is a later deviation caused by outside contamination of this original gospel truth. What is earlier is better than what is later. Tertullian contrasts the unity and simplicity of those foundations with the division and diversity of the heretics and their speculations. By the fourth century, this position had become basic to the normative master story of Christian origins and history.[46] It remained largely unchallenged until the work of Walter Bauer in 1934.[47] It is therefore a considerable irony that Tertullian, who provided the foundational paradigm for combating heresy, was himself later condemned as a heretic. But Tertullian's position remains one of the primary rhetorical modes for claiming power for oneself or one's group, and for excluding others.

So in the Jesus Seminar we too need to be careful not to take up this part of Tertullian's rhetoric — or let others claim we do — arguing that we are right because our Jesus is earlier, and therefore more authentic and pure. To do so would again allow those who wish to, to claim for themselves the power to say who are true Christians and who are heretics, the power to define the terms of the discourse.

The mere establishment of a data base makes no such claims. Critics have conveniently ignored the fact that scholars belonging to the Seminar have constructed some very different portraits of Jesus,[48] most of them having little to do with the Jesus ascribed to us (that is, described for us) by our critics. Similarly, to say, as we do, that the virgin birth or the physical resurrection are not historical actualities, understood in the terms of modern biological science, is not the end of the story. To concede that these are "facts that speak for themselves" would be to agree with the crassest positivism. Or as Marcus Borg put it, to acknowledge that we are indeed fact fundamentalists, who claim that there are only two choices: either the Bible is all true factually or Christianity is a lie. Such false choices cannot be allowed to define our faith, and Marcus shows us why and what to do in the move past critical engagement to a second naïveté.

But indeed there is always the danger of falling into Fundamentalism, even if it is based on a new, more historically reliable data base. If that data base were to become by us or by others the foundation for a new exclusive and authoritarian dogmatism, then the Fundamentalists will have won anyway. If that data base is claimed to represent the true, original Jesus against which all other claims to authentic Christianity must be measured, then dogmatism will be left quite in good order. But the data base alone can not and does not make such a claim. Nor did the early churches. Nor do we.

So here is the danger: to use the data base as itself a weapon of dogma to slay all who disagree with its contents. Now, I do not see us doing this, but I do see our opponents fearing that we are or at least that we will, quite possibly because it's what many of them do. Insofar as people claim their canon, their creed, their interpretation of scriptures, or indeed their very right to interpret scripture to be exclusive, they are claiming power — and it is this they fear might be taken away, the Guild as much as the churches.

The second discourse concerns the way in which Christian definition and self-definition are constructed in relation to Others. To understand oneself in terms of differentiation is not itself a problem. Indeed, as Jonathan Z. Smith points out, "when we confront difference we do not encounter irrationality or bad faith, but rather the very essence of thought. Meaning is made possible by difference."[49] Such thought "results in an object no longer natural but rather social, no longer factual but rather intellectual."[50] Christianity, in birthing itself as a socially and intellectually discrete entity, was defined to a large degree in terms of "Judaism." This "Judaism" was not a "natural" object, but was created as a dynamic and ever-changing entity suitable for Christian projects and politics of normative self-definition. As Smith puts it: "For in each case, a theory of difference, when applied to the proximate 'other,' is but another way of phrasing a theory of 'self'."[51]

Processes of defining the relationship of Judaism to Christianity are thoroughly entangled in the discourses of Christian identity politics. My own work on early Christian heresy[52] and the work of Daniel Boyarin on Jewish and Christian origins,[53] have suggested that both Jews and Christians were in the process of defining themselves, not solely in terms of inner-Jewish or inner-Christian debate and controversy, but also in relation to each other. There exists a Christian construction of "Judaism" (or rather a loosely conjoined set of constructions) whose main purpose is to aid in setting the normative boundaries of Christianity. Daniel Boyarin has argued that something similar can be said for Judaism's construction of "Christianity." Insofar as normativity is never a final state, but always in the process of formation, deformation, and reformation, it is possible to trace the interactions of Judaism and Christianity as sometimes parallel and reciprocal processes of identity/border construction.[54]

There are two foundational points here. First, that Judaism, Christianity, or indeed Hinduism or Islam, or any other such entity, are constructed and highly contested categories. Who gets to say what they are, who is in and who is out, what constitutes their "true essence" or orthodox dogma and practice — these are all highly political and constantly contested.

A second point is that struggles over self-definition involve how to define the Other, as well as Self. Christians have long engaged in this enterprise with regard to Judaism, constructing a Judaism suitable for Christian purposes and Christian polemics. One facile and highly dangerous way this is often done — too often — is to construct "Judaism" solely out of the rhetorical opponents of Jesus or Paul in the New Testament canon. Or again, to affirm that Jesus, Mary of Magdala, and Paul were Jews, but then simultaneously treat them as Christians over against Judaism.

The way this discourse of Self and Other plays out in the debates around the historical Jesus is illustrated effectively in charges about who "really" understands "Jesus the Jew." Rabbi and Professor Sandy Lowe, a member of the Seminar, has pointed me toward a new book by Susanna Heschel on modern views of the Jewish Jesus. She concludes that:

> the dispute over Jesus' religious identity . . . has never been resolved. As both a Jew and as the first Christian, yet neither fully a Jew nor a Christian, Jesus' uncertain religious identity has given rise to theological debates over the differences between the two religions. Jews dress him as a Jew, Christians dress him as a Christian, making him a figure on the boundary of the two religions. . . . For Judaism and Christianity, Jesus functions as a kind of literary transvestite, through which each religion inscribes the other, trying to define its relation to him.[55]

The debates over Jesus as eschatological prophet or Galilean sage seem, however, to have less to do with Christian-Jewish relations as such — however much such relations are indeed affected by these debates — than with the internal politics of Christian normativity. The question is whether this debate about Jesus as prophet or sage has much to do with Judaism at all, or whether it is rather a matter of Christians fighting for a particular construction of "Judaism" useful for particular Christian theologies. As our discussion of Bultmann illustrated, eschatology has become a site where a lot of Christian theological labour is performed, some of which I find sound and engaging.[56] But now it would appear that some scholars feel that the defense of such theology has to be based in the historical Jesus as an eschatological prophet or it loses its validity.

The fact that "apocalyptic eschatology" was generally disparaged as "particularistic" and "mythological" in earlier and explicitly anti-Semitic scholarship[57] is deployed rhetorically to imply that denying Jesus was an eschatological prophet makes one complicit with the old anti-Semitic stance. To argue in favor of this reconstruction of an eschatalogical Jesus implies rhetorically that one has slipped the bonds of Christian anti-Judaism. But is that enough actually to have done so?

Scholars who charge that the Seminar's portrait of Jesus as a Jewish sage is tantamount to inventing a non-Jewish Jesus seem to be suggesting that apocalyptic eschatology was an "essential" characteristic of the Judaism of Jesus' day, at least in Judaea-Palestine, such that any scholar who does not reconstruct Jesus this way is suspect.[58] Do these scholars mean to imply that any Jew who does not fully accept "the apocalyptic worldview" is not really Jewish? This puts modern historians in the position of selecting and defining a normative Judaism out of the variety of ancient Judaisms for which we have evidence, both within and outside of Judaea-Palestine.[59] It is questionable, to say the very least, whether this construction of Judaism for inner-Christian purposes and polemics is an adequate response or antidote to Christian anti-Judaism.

I do not believe that the Jesus Seminar has gotten out of this problem of viewing "Judaism" in terms constructed to serve Christian purposes, which is so characteristic of the field of New Testament generally. But it is simply false to say that because we have argued that Jesus' teaching was not centrally concerned with the future coming of the kingdom, was not expressed primarily in terms of apocalyptic-mythic language, that we have invented a non-Jewish Jesus. The Seminar has always assumed that Jesus was a Jew, and thus any Jesus we "found" would be a Jewish Jesus. The question is rather how to place Jesus within and among the Judaisms of his time and place.

Here, however, we would do well to listen to at least one of our critics. My new and dear colleague Krister Stendahl has made a somewhat different point in his repeated charges that the Seminar has constructed a non-Jewish Jesus. By not putting "common wisdom" (i.e., things that are attributed to Jesus, but are not distinctive to him, that were evidentially said and done by others) into the red or pink category, he argues that we have made a Jesus that is too distinctive, who has slipped too far from his mooring within his own intellectual and social world. Such a method runs the danger of plotting Jesus against Judaism, of inventing an historical figure who was part of no particular place or time. It is an important caution, and one we would do well to heed. But it is not particularly a reason to criticize the Seminar's process or its results in terms of the data base. Rather it constitutes a charge to take quite seriously all the gray material, the category in which we deposited much of the material that demonstrates a continuity of Jesus with his surroundings.[60] We should take this charge not to exaggerate artificially the gap between Jesus and his contemporaries — even if we still hear his voice in the crowd. It is a voice among other Jews, not apart from them.

My point, however, is not about the adequacy of the Seminar's data base. That question is far from settled, even within the Seminar itself. Engagement with the historical reconstruction of Jesus and early Christian formation is an ongoing task. The point I want to make here is that the old discourses, in which authentic Christian normativity is defined, in terms of the reconstruction of origins or the invention of a usable "Judaism," are inadequate. There is no necessary reason why the study of the historical Jesus must be about the politics of origins and authenticity, and there is every reason why the construction of "useful others" is not useful for "getting along."

What would alternatives to these discourses look like? And what role does historical inquiry play?

Writing Histories of Christianity in a Pluralistic World

It is clear that the study of the formative centuries of Christianity is potentially fruitful for reflection about many contemporary concerns. The Mediterranean world in which Christianity appeared was in a period of rapid social change and religious experimentation. It was a period in which traditional values and ways of life were being challenged and reshaped through contact with others; in which the family, gender roles, and sexuality were redefined; in which local resistances to Roman rule often took religious form, whether by outright rebellion as in the Jewish revolts in Palestine, or more covertly—for example, by turning a crucified criminal into a heroic symbol of resistance to worldly power and tyranny. It was a time in which a "new cult" (Christianity) moved from the margins of society to become the official religion of the Roman empire. Such a period offers a lot of issues to think about and a lot of material to think with.

Rethinking the history of this period is especially important for contemporary Christian communities, given the fact that quite often ideals of what Christianity should be, especially among Protestants, have been shaped by appeals to the early church. The time of origins is taken as a model for the present and the future. As a result, it is crucial how the story of Christian beginnings is told.

The beginning is often portrayed as the ideal moment to which all Christians and all of Christianity should aspire and conform. Here Jesus spoke to his disciples. Here the gospel was preached in truth. Here the churches were formed in the power of the Spirit. Here Christians lived in unity and love with one another. Here the mission was clear, and hard faith was forged in the fires of persecution.

What happens if we now tell this story differently? What if at the very beginning there were times of grappling and experimentation? What if the meaning of the gospel was not so clear? What if Christian communities struggled with trying to understand who Jesus was, what his violent death might mean? What if there were not unity and certainty at the beginning? What if Christians differed in their views and experiences, and sometimes came into conflict and division? What if the earliest Christian communities don't model for us a fixed and certain path, but instead call us to share in their struggles to make Christianity in our day, in our own communities, our nation and the world? What if idealized views of early Christianity, masquerading as impartial historical reconstruction, often function as tools in a politics of legitimation? What if Christianity in every age is being constructed anew? What might beginnings tell us then?

The final answer to these questions lies somewhere in the future. We are only beginning to construct a fuller and more accurate narrative of Christian beginnings. At this point I can only say that it will be a story of diverse groups of people engaged in the difficult business of working out what it means to be a Christian in a world of rapid social change, increased inter-cultural contact, and dominated overall by Roman imperial power. The story will talk about the issues that concerned them, their differences of opinion, the debates they had, and the solutions they devised, both successes and failures. It will portray some of them as pretty radical social experimenters, and others as more willing to compromise with the values of the dominant cultures. It will talk about the kind of communities they formed, about the utopian ideals of a loving God they nourished, and the burning desire for justice and for revenge that moved their imaginations. It will not be a secular story; it will talk about the force of religious faith to change the shape of the known world, and it will explore the limits of their vision and their experience for contemporary Christians.

This story of Christian beginnings — or rather *these stories*, for there is likely to be more than one — is in my opinion necessary for the vitality of contemporary Christian life. It may be that complex and impartial histories of Christian beginnings could lead to critical and constructive reflection on our own theologies and practices in their specifically contemporary contexts, of wealth and poverty, of privilege and deprivation, of natural beauty and environmental disaster, of truth and injustice. They could open up new possibilities for appreciating the diversity of forms that modern Christianity has taken globally, and for how Christianity has been enriched through contact with a wide variety of cultures in its 2000 year history. Understanding how Christianity was shaped by contact with others might help provide critical and constructive approaches to contemporary pluralism and inter-religious dialogue. One does not have to do more than read newspaper headlines in order to realize the need for us to come to terms with the multitude of religions' roles in society and politics, both for tremendous violence, but also for justice and peace. Historical study can help complexify the ways in which we think about such issues.

But the issue, too, is that there are serious problems with ignoring historical criticism for appropriation. By appropriation, I mean the life one leads, the degree to which the stories and practices of the Christian tradition (globally conceived) are fully incorporated (embodied) in that communal, social, political, and spiritual life.

The first problem is that ignoring historical criticism introduces a lie into any contemporary Christian faith that claims history as its basis. *It is not acceptable to claim that one's views are historically accurate and at the same time reject the standards and practices of historical method and historical thinking.* Such a lie undermines Christian practice and spirituality, which I assume has to do with truth and the real. Second, such a rejection of historical method has too often led to the intellectual impoverishment of Christian thought. Equally important, rejection of historical method precludes or at least seriously diminishes the capacity of communities of faith for critique and self-critique as a basis for theological reflection and liberating praxis. Such ignorance and refusal for conscious criticism in the face of religion's involvement in overt violence and injustice is morally wrong, and it is dangerous.

Let me give an example from my own work on Mary Magdalene and the *Gospel of Mary*.[61]

As many of you no doubt know, in Western European art and literature, Mary Magdalene is most often portrayed as a repentant prostitute, the Christian model of female sexuality redeemed. Yet there is not a single shred of reliable historical evidence to support that portrait.

To the contrary, the earliest Christian literature from the first century, including the canonical New Testament gospels, agrees in portraying Mary Magdalene as a prominent disciple of Jesus. She was a Jewish woman from the town of Magdala, located on the west shore of the Sea of Galilee, just north of the city of Tiberias.[62] Of independent means, she accompanied Jesus during his ministry[63] and supported him out of her own resources.[64] After his death she experienced visions of Jesus. According to the New Testament gospels, she was present at his crucifixion,[65] and was a witness to the resurrection.[66] Indeed, she is portrayed as the first or among the first privileged to see and speak with the risen Lord.[67]

What are we to make of this? If there is no basis in the Christian canon for the portrait of Mary Magdalene as a prostitute, where did the portrait of her as a repentant whore come from?

One key to this story is the Coptic literature discovered over the last centuries from Egypt.[68] Between 1773 and 1945, a series of remarkable discoveries in Egypt yielded a set of papyrus books containing a number of works in which Mary Magdalene figured prominently, including the only surviving copy of the early second century *Gospel of Mary (Magdalene)*.[69] Together these works offer some important insights into the social and political dynamics that catalyzed the creation of the fictive portrait of Mary Magdalene as a repentant prostitute and they offer an alternative portrait of her.

Despite considerable variety in content, this literature is consistent in developing the early first century portrait of Mary Magdalene as a visionary and leading apostle, sometimes even as Jesus' favored disciple. Her role as 'apostle to the apostles' is frequently explored, especially in considering her faith in contrast to that of the male disciples who refuse to believe her testimony. The strength of this literary tradition, especially its multiple attestation, makes it possible to suggest that historically Mary may have been a prophetic visionary and leader within some sector of the early Christian movement after the death of Jesus.

The literature, however, clearly goes beyond history to elaborate richly on Mary's story. Much like the legendary afterlife of other disciples in works like the *Acts of Thomas* or the *Apocalypse of Paul*, the prestige of apostolic lineage serves as a guarantor of the truth of the teachings associated with her or them. But the teachings that came to be associated with Mary's name were connected with views that lost out, at least partially, in the battles for Christianity. While the *Gospel of Mary* does affirm that Jesus lived and died as a human being, it mentions his death only as the occasion for the disciples to overcome their own quite real and realistic fear of death in preaching the gospel. It is not Jesus' death, but understanding and appropriating Jesus' teaching that is crucial for salvation. Ancient Christians were agreed that Jesus' death and resurrection were a reality; they were also agreed that his experience would be model for their own. Where they disagreed was on the nature of that resurrection: was it the resuscitation of a physical corpse (and hence all believers would also experience resuscitation), or the transformation of the physical body into a spiritual body (an experience that would occur only to believers, while unbelievers would simply remain dead), or was it the separation of the soul from the body and its elevation to life with God? And what was a soul anyway? There was a great deal at stake for issues of authority and ethics in how these questions were answered. In denying that the physical body is the true self destined for life with God, the *Gospel of Mary* was able to argue that the basis for leadership lay in a person's spiritual maturity, not any ephemeral physical characteristic like gender or sexuality. Mary exemplifies the ideal: she remained firm where others feared and doubted; she received special prophetic and visionary wisdom from Jesus, where others had not yet comprehended his basic teachings; she stepped in to comfort and teach others, not because she had a right but because they had need. Men and women were to exercise leadership based on this kind of spiritual understanding and attainment.[70] Women could exercise leadership on the basis of spiritual achievement apart from gender status and without conformity to established social gender roles.

It may therefore be no coincidence that these teachings were pseudonymously attributed to a prominent woman. That that woman was Mary Magdalene reflects both her prominence in early gospel literature and her probable leadership in early Christianity. It also charts one possible path in her legendary afterlife. In contrast, the church fathers, whose writings later become the basis for orthodoxy, largely ignore Mary Magdalene in the early centuries, although when they do mention her, the fathers also present her in a consistently favorable light.[71]

From the fourth century onward, however, as Christianity became the religion of a world empire rather than an elicit and persecuted practice, the tone began to shift.[72] Why? The close association of the name of Mary Magdalene with a kind of theological reflection that was later rejected provides a new clue as to why the portrait of Mary Magdalene as prostitute was invented. Discrediting her may have been in part a strategy of the church fathers to counter the interpretation of

Jesus' teaching, and the arguments for women's leadership which were being spread in works like the *Gospel of Mary*.[73]

Silence, it turned out, was not an effective strategy, for it left the imaginative field open to others. So starting in the fourth century, Christian theologians in the Latin West invented an alternative story. (It should be noted that the Eastern Churches never made this error.) The confusion began by associating Mary Magdalene with the unnamed sinner woman who anointed Jesus' feet in Luke 7:36–50; then conflating that account with John 12:1–8, in which Mary of Bethany anoints Jesus. From this point, the move to identifying Mary of Magdala with Mary of Bethany was a short one. Once this initial identification was secured, Mary Magdalene could be associated with every unnamed sinful woman in the gospels, including the adulteress in John 8:1–11 and the Syrophoenician woman with her five and more "husbands" in John 4:7–30.[74]

At the end of the sixth century, Pope Gregory the Great gave a sermon in which he not only identified these figures, but drew the moral conclusion that would dominate the imagination of the West for centuries to come:

> She whom Luke calls the sinful woman, whom John calls Mary, we believe to be the Mary from whom seven devils were ejected according to Mark. And what did these seven devils signify, if not all the vices? ... It is clear, brothers, that the woman previously used the unguent to perfume her flesh in forbidden acts. What she therefore displayed more scandalously, she was now offering to God in a more praiseworthy manner. She had coveted with earthly eyes, but now through penitence these are consumed with tears. She displayed her hair to set off her face, but now her hair dries her tears. She had spoken proud things with her mouth, but in kissing the Lord's feet, she now planted her mouth on the Redeemer's feet. For every delight, therefore, she had had in herself, she now immolated herself. She turned the mass of her crimes to virtues, in order to serve God entirely in penance, for as much as she had wrongly held God in contempt.[75]

Mary the apostle and teacher had become Mary the repentant whore.

In the end, out of the same sacred texts, two basic portraits of Mary Magdalene were developed: one that stressed her roles as a prominent disciple of Jesus, a visionary, and a spiritual teacher; the other that painted her as a repentant prostitute whom Jesus forgave, a latter-day Eve turned from her sinful ways.[76] The story of the repentant prostitute ruled the imagination of the West for over a millennium. Now the earlier and more historical portrait is being recovered and is replacing that of the repentant whore. Out of imagination of twentieth century women scholars are arising images of a woman who was a strong prophetic visionary and an apostolic leader.

What does this story of Mary Magdalene from apostle to prostitute and back again tell us about the complexities in the relationship between sacred texts and social contexts?

To begin, there is no one-to-one relationship between text and social practice. Despite rhetorical claims to the contrary, texts do not have a single true meaning nor do they function like rules. Sacred texts and the myths they contain do not predetermine a people's behavior, but rather provide an orientation for improvisation and its limits. The figure of Mary Magdalene and narratives about her can be elaborated in any number of directions, and used to think about a variety of topics, such as what it means to be a follower of Jesus, about the body and salvation, about the qualities of leadership, and so on. Reference to her can be used to locate the nature and cause of sin in femaleness or the sexuality associated with her; it can be used to illustrate the magnanimity of God in transforming sin into purity through acts of suffering, penance and self-denial; it can be used to authorize women's public speech and prophetic power, or even public leadership over men; and so on. Such references can be improvised in limitless and contradictory ways without ever departing from a consensus about the sacred texts. Everyone can agree on the basic content of the New Testament narratives about Mary Magdalene and yet she can nonetheless be a figure around which considerable controversy brews.

Evidence is not sufficient to change an interpretation of sacred texts. How they are read is not merely a function of what they say. The material context, the social relations, who has access to texts and to the authorized modes of interpreting texts, the rhetorical-political functions sacred texts serve — all are crucial to the construction of their meaning in practice. As those contexts and institutions shift, so does meaning. The fact that the traditions about Mary the prostitute can today be rejected and replaced with an apostolic leader has little to do with the new evidence from Egypt. It has much more to do with new technologies of reproduction, the increasing numbers of women in the workforce, the civil rights and women's movements, more and more women earning advanced degrees, and so on. Such a history illustrates that not only what sacred texts say, but who is authorized to interpret them is crucial for their functioning meanings in practice.

Religious tradition, even sacred texts, are not static givens, but always in ongoing processes of formation. It is critical to shift the usual perspective away from understanding "religions as ready-made systems of meaning awaiting interpretation" to the view that "people are spinning what Geertz called 'webs of meaning' all the time, with whatever cultural resources happen to be at hand."[77] The fundamental assumption we need to work with is that "people are always trying to make sense of their lives, always weaving fabrics of meaning, however fragile and fragmentary."[78] The processes of meaning-making belong to the normal, everyday operations of living and are performed by all people.

Tradition is not simply the unchanged materials handed down from the past,[79] rather people living in the present decide on and indeed fight for what will constitute their true tradition.[80] In doing so, they appropriate some elements of the past and reject others. Even the elements of the past that are kept take on new meanings by being deployed in new or changing contexts.

The most important point, and the only one I will insist on, is that people are responsible for the ways in which sacred texts and sacred stories are selected, composed, read, and used. If the texts matter at all, have any real place in the practices of meaning-making and belonging, then how one interprets and uses the texts needs to be subjected to considered, collective, and critical reflection.

The *Sitz im Leben* for this process, now as in the formational period, is community. Here we do well to listen to the words and the wisdom of the Jewish feminist theologian Judith Plaskow:

> The contrary uses to which the Bible has been put suggest that the needs and values of a community of readers are as much a source of norms as the texts themselves . . . itself is a product of community. It may be revelatory or communicate lasting values, but revelation is communally received and molded . . . (The authority of the Bible is grounded in) the experience of particular communities struggling for religious transformation. . . . To name this community as my authority is to call it the primary community to which I am accountable.[81]

This formulation of Scripture and tradition as authority in community is both sound historically, replicating as it does the foundational formation of religions, and theologically, acknowledging as it does the moral responsibilities and ethical implications of belonging to a religious community. To locate this process in community is not to claim revelation lies in the church rather than with Jesus. It is to break with this dichotomy and locate human connection with God in relation to one another and to the world. Appeals to New Testament canon as a time-less source of unchanging Truth obscure both the living processes of religious faith and practice, and suffocate human responsibility under the cloak of authoritarianism.

Robert Funk asked us whether we think Christianity will sur-vive into the next millennium. Globally there is no doubt of that. Christianity is, for example, the fastest growing religion in Africa. But the answer for us may rest upon whether or not we live out of and appropriate these stories and how. It would be the failure to do so that would signal the end of Christianity and the relevance of Jesus in our own time and place. The teachings of Jesus will thrive. The question is who will tell those stories? What will they mean? How will they be lived? What lessons will we learn from our sisters and brothers in other contexts? What will we fight about?

Concluding Reflections

The world at the end of the twentieth century requires that we think differently about the questions of what it means to be a Christian, about what Christianity is, and who decides. Harnack's vision of Christianity as a bodiless being of the air hovering over the earth, "bodiless and seeking a body," is not possible for us. No more can we envision schol-ars as transcendent beings hovering over the texts, presuppositionless and seeking objectivity. Rather meaning is constituted only in particular social contexts and practices. We no longer can think of Judaism as the "background" against which Christianity's "essence" distinguishes itself, but as the world in which particular historical persons, Jesus, Mary of Magdala, Paul, and Junia lived and thought and acted wholly and fully. Similarly our scholarly quests are positioned[82] as we are, in particular but constantly shifting contexts and practices.

What is left to historicized historians when the transcendent essence of Christianity is gone? What is left, I suggest, is the history of Christianity itself. Such an account would not privilege beginnings, but would include all the information about Christianity everywhere across time: Ethiopian Christianity, Christianity on the Malabar Coast of India, Eastern Orthodoxy, Nestorianism, Coptic Christianity, African diaspora Christianities, the European Reformations and Counter-

Reformations, 19th century US Evangelical Christianities, Christianity in Hong Kong, in Latin American, in the Philippines, and elsewhere. Christianity historically as all its parts, all its stories, all its practices and the experiences of all men and women, of all races and geographical locations, across all cultural and linguistic homes. Not in their totality, as though some new totalizing narrative will ever capture them, but in their pluriformity and historical particularities.

Embracing this view of tradition offers histories of Christianity as a rich heritage from which to draw for inspiration, instruction, and critique. It will provide many more resources for critical thought and practice than the limitations of creed and canon now supply. History is not able to settle the issue of Christian identity — that is up to Christian communities — but it can provide corrective information about the history of the creation of Christian "essence." It is possible to identify and critically engage historically the forces at work in the creation and recreation ("maintenance") of Christian beliefs and practices. The stakes are high.

Such a position, however, only aggravates questions about theological normativity. The Preacher of Ecclesiastes tells us that "God has put eternity into the human mind, yet so that people cannot find out what God has done from the beginning to the end."[83] We live, it would seem, between time and eternity. My insistence on shifting meanings may stir a nostalgia for a lost objectivity, fixed certainly, the truth and justice that is divine. But we live in a mortal sphere, situated in very specific times and shifting contexts. We live between the certainty of divine truth and the uncertainty of human knowledge and action, except perhaps for the certainty of our own human imperfection and finitude. Yet I for one am not nostalgic for a return to the fantasies of pure objectivity, for between time and eternity lies the possibility, or perhaps I should say, the necessity for human responsibility, creativity, humility.

Notes

1. *What is Christianity*, 56.
2. *What is Christianity*, 56.
3. *What is Christianity*, 54.
4. See *What is Christianity*, 55–56.
5. *What is Christianity*, 8.
6. *What is Christianity*, 51.
7. *What is Christianity*, 193.
8. See Funk et al., *The Parables of Jesus*; McGaughy, "The Search for the Historical Jesus."
9. Translated into English as *The Gospel and the Church*.

10. It is symptomatic that Loisy consistently speaks not of (the historical) Jesus, but of Christ (the messiah).
11. *The Gospel and the Church*, 13.
12. *The Gospel and the Church*, 18–19.
13. Loisy writes, for example: "The mission of Christ is not presented in the Gospels in this primitive form. Tradition must follow its natural tendency, and was soon to discover, in the ministry of Jesus, characteristic features and indubitable proofs of His Messianic dignity" (*The Gospel and the Church*, 38).
14. *The Gospel and the Church*, 10.
15. See *History of Dogma* I, 47.
16. *The Gospel and the Church*, 65.
17. *The Gospel and the Church*, 54.
18. *The Gospel and the Church*, 11
19. See *The Gospel and the Church*, 10–11.
20. Bultmann wrote: "Harnack somehow never clearly saw nor understood the eschatological character of the appearance of Jesus and of his preaching of the immanent advent of the Kingdom of God. Moreover, Harnack never gave due consideration to the eschatological consciousness with which the early Christian communities and Paul were suffused. In fact, Harnack never even caught a glimpse of the utter strangeness of the image of primitive Christianity disclosed by the religious-historical school, and which even today at first inevitably shocks a reader of the New Testament" (Introduction," x).
21. Bultmann, *Jesus and the Word*, 38.
22. Note Bultmann's reference to Schweitzer in "Introduction," x, n. 5.
23. Bultmann, "Introduction," x.
24. Bultmann, *Jesus and the Word*, 43.
25. Bultmann, *Jesus and the Word*, 47.
26. Bultmann, *Jesus and the Word*, 39.
27. Bultmann, *Jesus and the Word*, 40–41.
28. Bultmann, *Jesus and the Word*, 51.
29. Bultmann, "Introduction," xi.
30. Harnack, *What is Christianity*, 149.
31. One must, however, read this "timeless man" with a hermeneutics of suspicion. It is no doubt the case that Harnack intended the term to be used "inclusively," but contemporary feminism has made it clear that the construction of "universal man" is far from inclusive, not only in terms of gender, but also sexuality, race, and class.
32. Harnack, *What is Christianity*, 62.
33. Certainly earlier generations had acknowledged the gap between the teachings of Jesus in the Gospels and the teachings about Jesus, for example in Paul. They, too, had noted that the gospels were the products of later Christians, and reflected their interests and perspectives. Scholars had long held that comparison of the Synoptic Gospels and John did not reflect favorably upon the latter's historical reliability in constructing the life and teachings of the historical Jesus. Indeed much New Testament scholarship has been concerned either obliquely or directly with determining what materials could reliably be traced back to oral tradition behind the written gospels, and what to Jesus himself.
34. For a balanced statement of the Seminar's understanding of its results, see Miller, *The Jesus Seminar and its Critics*, 76.
35. See again the treatment of this issue by Miller, *The Jesus Seminar and its Critics*, 125–46.

36. See *The Five Gospels*, 3–5.
37. These issues are better addressed in the Seminar's papers and especially by Miller, *The Jesus Seminar and its Critics*, 71–76.
38. Clifford Geertz, "The world in pieces: culture and politics at the end of the century." *Focaal* 32 (1998), 96.
39. A phrase borrowed from the beautiful memoirs of Leila Ahmed, *A Border Passage*, 296.
40. *Prescriptions against Heretics* 7 (p. 36).
41. See *Prescriptions against Heretics* 13.
42. See *Prescriptions against Heretics* 20–21, 32.
43. *Prescriptions against Heretics* 20 (p. 43–44).
44. *Prescriptions against Heretics* 31 (p. 52).
45. *Prescriptions against Heretics* 35 (p. 56).
46. See, for example, the plot of Eusebius' *Church History*.
47. See Bauer, *Rechtgläubigkeit und Ketzerie im ältesten Christentum* (1934); translated into English as *Orthodoxy and Heresy in Earliest Christianity* (1971).
48. E.g., Borg, *Meeting Jesus Again*; Crossan, *The Historical Jesus*; Funk, *Honest to Jesus*; Hedrick, *When History and Faith Collide*; Patterson, *The God of Jesus*.
49. Smith, "Differential Equations," 14.
50. Smith, "Differential Equations," 14.
51. Smith, "Differential Equations," 14.
52. See, for example, "The Politics of Syncretism and the Problem of Defining Gnosticism." Church historians therefore have tended to distinguish the two major types of the earliest heresy based on the relationship of Christianity to Judaism: Jewish Christianity appropriates too much Judaism and/or takes too positive an attitude toward it; Gnosticism appropriates too little and/or takes too negative an attitude. "Orthodoxy" apparently sails between this Scylla and Charybdis, safe from both dangers. Properly defining the relationship of Judaism to Christianity is the crux of scholarly efforts at categorizing the types of heresy in the formative period. What this distinction does rhetorically, therefore, is point toward the relationship of Christianity to Judaism as one of the most important factors, if not the single most important factor, in the modern discourse of "orthodoxy and heresy" (or the bounds of normativity) deployed in defining authentic Christianity. No doubt the proximity of Judaism as a living tradition is a factor of some importance in this emphasis.
53. E.g. his essay on "When Christians Were Jews: On Judaeo-Christian Origins" (manuscript).
54. For further discussion of this topic, see King, "Rethinking the (Jewish) Origins of (Christian) Gnosticism."
55. Heschel, *Abraham Geiger and the Jewish Jesus*, 239.
56. Especially the work of Schüssler Fiorenza on Revelations (see, for example, "The Followers of the Lamb").
57. Such a portrait is, however, much more complicated than this simple sentence allows. For example, Harnack's denigration of Judaism is assumed rather than the active object of his work. It is true that Harnack, while acknowledging Jesus' "background" in "Late Judaism" (as he styles it), at the same time insisted that the essence of Christianity is not historical (see *What is Christianity?* xiii, 13–14, 54, 124, 129–30, 149,187, 191). He goes so far as to insist that "none of the forms in which (the Gospel)

assumed intellectual and social expression — not even the earliest — can be regarded as possessing a classical and permanent character"(*What is Christianity?* 191). So, on the one hand, Harnack rejects not only the connection with Judaism, but also with Hellenism — or *any other possible intellectual-social matrix* — as capable of expressing the full "essence of Christianity." In this sense, rejecting Judaism is not especially the object of Harnack's insistence on the distinctive character of Christianity.

58. See, for example, Pearson, "The Gospel According to the Jesus Seminar," 18, who suggests that anyone who does not read the historical Jesus in terms of "the apocalyptic worldview" of first-century Palestine, can be supposed to have a "'hidden agenda.'"

59. Accessible statements of this variety can be found in Overman and Green, "Judaism (Greco-Roman Period)" and Fraade, "Judaism (Palestinian)."

60. See Miller, *The Jesus Seminar and its Critics*, 52–53. See also Kea, "Finding a Voice for the Black Sayings."

61. Portions of this paper, especially in this section, were previously presented at the Harvard University Divinity School Convocation, Cambridge, Massachusetts, September, 1999, and will appear in my forthcoming book on *The Gospel of Mary*.

62. See Jane Schaberg's account of visiting the present location in "Thinking Back through the Magdalene."

63. See *Mark* 15:40–41; *Matthew* 27:55–56; *Luke* 8:1–3; *John* 19:25; *Gospel of Philip* 59.6–9(?).

64. See *Luke* 8:1–3; Ricci, *Mary Magdalene and Many Others*; Haskins, *Mary Magalene*, p. 14.

65. *Mark* 15:40–41; *John* 19:25. She was also said to be present at the entombment in *Mark* 15:47 and *Matthew* 27:61.

66. *Mark* 16:1–8; *Matthew* 28:1–7; *Luke* 24:1–10; *John* 20:1, 11–13. The *Gospel of Peter* also gives Mary Magdalene a preeminent place as the first witness to the empty tomb, although the material about Mary may be a secondary addition, influenced by the New Testament gospel tradition (see Crossan, *The Cross that Spoke*, 285–86).

67. *Matthew* 28:9–10; *John* 20:14–18; *Mark* 16:9. See also the *Epistulum Apostolorum*. In the *Gospel of John*, the risen Jesus gives her special teaching and commissions her as an apostle to the apostles to bring them the good news (*John* 20:17). In *Mark* 16:17 and *Matthew* 28:7, angels commission Mary and the other women to carry the news of the resurrection. Among the earliest Christian art that survives are portraits of Mary Magdalene with other women bringing spices to the tomb to anoint Jesus. (See Milburn, *Early Christian Art and Architecture*, 12; Haskins, *Mary Magdalene*, 58–63).

68. For further discussion of this material, see King, "The Gospel of Mary (Magdalene)" in *Searching the Scriptures*; "The Gospel of Mary" in *The Complete Gospels*; Marjanen, *The Woman Jesus Loved*.

69. *Gospel of Mary* BG 19:5; her name appears also at BG 9:12, 20–21; 10:1, 7; 17:7; 18:1; POxy 3525, 8–9[*], 13[*], 15, 17; PRyl 463, 3.

70. For further discussion of the *Gospel of Mary*, see King, "The Gospel of Mary (Magdalene)" in *Searching the Scriptures*; "Prophetic Power and Women's Authority."

71. See Corley, "'Noli me tangere'," (unpublished manuscript); Haskins, *Mary Magdalene*, 58–67, 90. Robert M. Price has argued that the tendency to diminish Mary's role as the first, and perhaps only, witness is already evidenced in the New Testament gospels and Paul (see Price, "Mary

Magdalene"). Yet she is rarely mentioned and then only in passing to support points they are trying to make about the reality of the physical resurrection (see, for example, Origen, *Against Celsus* 2) or the nature of the soul (see Tertullian, *De Anima*, 25.8). Tertullian uses the report that Mary was possessed by seven demons to support his view (that a child possesses soul from the moment of conception) by showing that it is possible for one person to have two souls (that is, the soul of the mother and the soul of the child).

Her name comes up most frequently in connection with the resurrected Jesus' enigmatic statement to her: "Do not touch me, for I have not yet ascended to the Father" (*John* 20.17), because the fathers were concerned to counter any impression this passage gives that Jesus' resurrection might not have been physical (see, for example, Irenaeus, *Against Heresies* 5.31; Origen *Commentary on John* 6.37; 10.21).

72. The fathers increasingly tended to explain Jesus' command not to touch him by arguing that Mary, unlike Thomas, was not worthy of touching the resurrected Lord because she lacked a full understanding of the resurrection and hence lacked true faith (for example, Ambrose *On the Christian Faith*, 4.2; Jerome, *To Pammachius Against John of Jerusalem* 35; Jerome, *To Marcella* 59.4; Augustine, *Sermon* 244.3). She was sent to the male apostles, it was argued, so that her weakness could be supplemented by their strength (Ambrose, cited from Haskins, *Mary Magdalen*, 93).

It was nonetheless appropriate, the fathers began to argue, that a woman be the first to receive the redemption offered by Jesus through his resurrection, because it was after all—at least in their interpretation of the Genesis story (for two alternative readings, see Trible, *God and the Rhetoric of Sexuality*; and King, "*The Book of Norea*") — a woman who had first brought sin into the world (see, for example, Gregory of Nyssa, *Contra Eunomium* 3.10; Augustine *Sermon* 232.2). References begin to appear to Mary Magdalene as the second Eve, the woman whose faith in the resurrected Jesus overcame the offenses of first Eve (see Ambrose, *Of the Holy Spirit* 3.11).

73. Or those in the *Dialogue of the Savior*, the *Sophia of Jesus Christ*, or the *Pistis Sophia*.

74. See Schaberg, "How Mary Magdalene Became a Whore."

75. Gregory, *Homily* 33 (quoted from Haskins, *Mary Magdalene*, 96).

76. There are cases in the Medieval period when these two portraits were combined. See Jansen, "Maria Magdalena."

77. Ortner, "Introduction," 9.

78. Ortner, "Introduction," 9.

79. "Thus we can no longer speak of tradition in terms of the approximate identity of some objective thing that changes while remaining the same. Instead, we must understand tradition as a symbolic process that both presupposes past symbolisms and creatively reinterprets them. In other words, tradition is not a bounded entity made up of bounded constituent parts, but a process of interpretation, attributing meaning in the present though making reference to the past" (Handler and Linnekin, "Tradition, Genuine or Spurious," 287).

80. As Handler and Linnekin put it: "In sum, traditions, thought to be preserved, are created out of the conceptual needs of the present. Tradition is not handed down from the past, as a thing or collection of things; it is

symbolically reinvented in an ongoing present" ("Tradition, Genuine or Spurious," 280.
81. Plaskow, *Standing Again at Sinai*, 19, 20, 21.
82. I would like this lone word, "positioned," to carry the full weight of current discussions of positionality, in terms of race, class, gender, geography, and other crucial factors that impact our social and intellectual activities. See, for example, Martin and Mohanty, "Feminist Politics."
83. Ecclesiatstes 3:10–15 (RSV)

Works Cited

Ahmed, Leila, *A Border Passage. From Cairo to America — A Woman's Journey*. New York: Farrar, Straus and Giroux, 1999.

Bauer, Walter, *Orthodoxy and Heresy in Earliest Christianity*. Philadelphia: Fortress Press, 1971.

Borg, Marcus J., *Meeting Jesus Again for the First Time. The Historical Jesus and the Heart of Contemporary Faith*. New York: HarperSanFrancisco, 1994.

Bultmann, Rudolf, "Introduction." Pp. vii–xviii in *What is Christianity?* by Adolf Harnack. New York: Harper and Row, 1957.

Bultmann, Rudolf, *Jesus and the Word*. New York: Charles Scribners, 1934.

Crossan, John Dominic, *The Cross that Spoke: The Origins of the Passion Narrative*. San Francisco: Harper and Row, 1988.

Crossan, John Dominic, *The Historical Jesus. The Life of a Mediterranean Jewish Peasant*. New York: HarperSanFrancisco, 1991.

Fraade, Steven D., "Judaism (Palestinian)." Pp. 1054–61 in *The Anchor Bible Dictionary* III. Ed. David Noel Freedman. New York: Doubleday, 1992.

Funk, Robert W., *Honest to Jesus. Jesus for a New Millennium*. New York: HarperSanFrancisco,1996.

Funk, Robert W., Roy W. Hoover, and the Jesus Seminar, *The Five Gospels. The Search for the Authentic Words of Jesus*. New York: MacMillan, 1993.

Funk, Robert W., Bernard Brandon Scott, and James R. Butts, *The Parables of Jesus. Red Letter Edition. A Report of the Jesus Seminar*. Sonoma, CA: Polebridge Press, 1988.

Geertz, Clifford, "The world in pieces: culture and politics at the end of the century." *Focaal* 32 (1998), pp 91–117.

Handler, Richard and Jocelyn Linnekin, "Tradition, Genuine or Spurious." *The Journal of American Folklore* 97 (1984), pp 273–90.

Harnack, Adolf von, *What is Christianity?* New York: Harper and Row, 1957.

Harnack, Adolph von, *The History of Dogma* (7 volumes). Trans. Neil Buchanan from the Third German Edition, c. 1900. New York: Dover Publications, 1961.

Haskins, Susan, *Mary Magalene. Myth and Metaphor*. New York, San Diego, and London: Harcourt Brace & Co., 1993.

Hedrick, Charles W., *When History and Faith Collide: Studying Jesus*. Peabody, MA: Hendrickson Publishers, 1999.

Heschel, Susanna, *Abraham Geiger and the Jewish Jesus*. Chicago: University of Chicago Press, 1998.

Jansen, Katherine Ludwig, "Maria Magdalena: *Apostolorum Apostola*." Pp. 57–96 in *Women Preachers and Prophets through Two Millennia of Christianity*. Ed. Beverly Mayne Kienzle and Pamela J.Walker. Berkeley and Los Angeles: University of California Press, 1998.

Kea, Perry V., "Finding a Voice for the Black Sayings." *The Fourth R* 8.5/6 (1995), 3–8.

King, Karen L.,"The Book of Norea, Daughter of Eve." Pp. 66–85 in *Searching the Scriptures. A Feminist Commentary.* Ed. Elisabeth Schüssler Fiorenza. New York: Crossroad, 1994.

King, Karen L., "The Gospel of Mary." Pp. 357–66 in *The Complete Gospels. Annotated Scholars Version.* Ed. Robert J. Miller. Rev. and ex. edition. Sonoma, CA: Polebridge Press, 1994.

King, Karen L., "The Gospel of Mary Magdalene." Pp. 601–34 in *Searching the Scriptures. II. A Feminist Commentary.* Ed. Elisabeth Schüssler Fiorenza. New York: Crossroads, 1994.

King, Karen L., "The Politics of Syncretism and the Problem of Defining Gnosticism." *Historical Reflections/Réflexions Historiques.* Volume ed. William Cassidy. Forthcoming.

King, Karen L., "Prophetic Power and Women's Authority: the Case of the Gospel of Mary Magdalene." Pp. 21–41 in *Women Preachers and Prophets through Two Millennia of Christianity.* Ed. Beverly Mayne Kienzle and Pamela J. Walker. Berkeley and Los Angeles: University of California Press, 1998.

King, Karen L., "Rethinking the (Jewish) Origins of (Christian) Gnosticism." *Journal of Early Christian Studies.* Volume ed., Daniel Boyarin. Submitted for review.

Loisy, Alfred, *The Gospel and the Church.* Philadelphia: Fortress Press, 1976.

Marjanen, Antti, *The Woman Jesus Loved. Mary Magdalene in the Nag Hammadi Library and Related Documents.* Nag Hammadi and Manichaean Studies XL. Leiden: E. J. Brill, 1996.

Martin, Biddy and Chandra Talpade, Mohanty, "Feminist Politics: What's Home Got to Do with It?" Pp. 195–212 in *Feminist Studies/Critical Studies.* Ed. Teresa de Laurentis. Bloomington: Indiana University Press, 1991.

McGaughy, Lane C., "The Search for the Historical Jesus. Why Start with the Sayings?" *The Fourth R* 9.5/6 (1996), pp 17–26.

Milburn, Robert, *Early Christian Art and Architecture.* Berkeley and Los Angeles: University of California Press, 1988.

Miller, Robert J., *The Jesus Seminar and Its Critics.* Santa Rosa, CA: Polebridge Press, 1999.

Ortner, Sherry B., "Introduction." *Representations* 59 (1997), pp 1–13.

Overman, J. Andrew and William Scott Green, "Judaism (Greco-Roman Period)." Pp. 1037–54 in *The Anchor Bible Dictionary* III. Ed. David Noel Freedman. New York: Doubleday, 1992.

Patterson, Stephen J., *The God of Jesus: The historical Jesus and the Search for Meaning.* Harrisburg, PA: Trinity Press International, 1998.

Pearson, Birger, "The Gospel According to the Jesus Seminar." *Occasional Papers* 35. Claremont, CA: Institute for Antiquity and Christianity, 1996. [A briefer version of this essay was published in *Religion* 25 (1995), pp 317–338.]

Plaskow, Judith, *Standing Again at Sinai. Judaism from a Feminist Perspective.* New York: HarperSanFrancisco, 1990.

Price, Robert M., "Mary Magdalene: Gnostic Apostle?" *Grail* 6.2 (1990), 54–76.

Ricci, Carla, *Mary Magdalene and Many Others. Women who followed Jesus.* Trans. Paul Burns. Minneapolis: Fortress Press, 1994.

Schaberg, Jane, "How Mary Magdalene Became a Whore." *Bible Review* 5 (1992), pp 30–37, 51–52.

Schaberg, Jane, "Thinking Back through the Magdalene." *Continuum* 1.2 (1991), 71–90

Schüssler Fiorenza, Elisabeth, "The Followers of the Lamb: Visionary Rhetoric and Social-Political Situation." *Semeia* 36 (1986), pp 123–46.

Smith, Jonathan Z., "Differential Equations: On Constructing the 'Other'." Thirteenth Annnual [sic] University Lecture in Religion. Arizona State University. March 5, 1992.

Tertullian, *Prescriptions Against Heretics*. Pp. 25–64 in *Early Latin Theology*. Trans. and ed. S. L. Greenslade. The Library of Christian Classics. Philadelphia: The Westminster Press, 1956.

Trible, Phyllis, *God and the Rhetoric of Sexuality*. Philadelphia: Fortress Press, 1978.

John Dominic Crossan

a Future for the
Christian Faith?

Our present seminar on "The Once and Future Jesus" explicitly involves questions not only about the future of Jesus but also about the future of faith and church. That invites me, as I see it, not only to speak about my own reconstruction of the historical Jesus but to imagine, based on that research, the future of Christianity itself. In this article, therefore, I move quite consciously between study and prophecy, I walk quite willingly along the borders of history, theology, and autobiography. My discussion will have three parts, on God (or, better, the Holy) as Trinity, on the historical Jesus and earliest Christianity as apocalyptic or non-apocalyptic, and on the Christian Church, but, as you may expect, I will spend most time on that middle section. I begin with a brief consideration of two presuppositions foundational for what follows.

The Aesopic Fallacy

The Aesopians are an ancient and venerable religious community going back in time over two and a half millennia. Their religion was founded by a Greek slave named Aesop and his book *The Fables* is accepted by all Aesopians as their inspired text of sacred scripture. They have recently been embroiled in a nasty public dispute which ended up in a very high-profile legal battle.

It began when a group called Scientists against Mythology described the Aesopians as a bunch of half-witted weirdos. The Aesopians immediately sued them under the new federal law forbidding hate-mockery of individuals for peculiarities of race, creed, color, ethnic origin, or physical challenge. (It was passed in Central Florida after somebody called Mickey Mouse an impotent rodent.) The obvious choice as lead-prosecutor was Johnny Cockroach but he was already involved as counsel for Bart Simpson before the House Committee on Un-American Family Activities (and besides, as he told the press, he did not have a word that rhymed with genre). The Aesopians chose, but as their reluctant second choice, a Boston-Irish lawyer named Póg Mahóney. He was brilliant, he was ruthless, he was devastating.

The first expert for the defense was a Pulitzer-prize-winning historian from Harvard. She was shredded on the stand as Mahóney insisted and the judge agreed that she must answer a simple Yes or No to the questions put to her. Were you alive in ancient Greece at the time of Aesop. No. Have you read all the extant documents from ancient Greece? Yes. Do you think that those represent all there ever were from that time? No. Then, Madam, since you do not know everything that happened in ancient Greece, is not your assertion that animal linguisticality did not occur there simply a personal historical bias?

The second expert was a Nobel-prize-winning biologist from Stanford but he too went down in flames. Are there changes in animal evolution so that earlier capabilities are later lost? Yes. (A whole series of forcibly-admitted examples followed with much debate about non-flying chickens.) Do you know, or does science know, every single species of presently-living animal? No. Could there be some animals even now, in the canopies of the rain forest or the depths of the sea, about which we know nothing, not even their existence? Yes. Then, Sir, since you do not know all past or even all contemporary animals, is it not fair to say that your assertion of their non-linguisticality is simply an individual prejudice?

The jury took only half an hour to find for the prosecution and to assess both compensatory and punitive damages amounting to fourteen million dollars. Both legal teams were mobbed by the media on the courtyard steps. What will you do next, the defense was asked? We are going all the way to the United States Supreme Court. What will you do next, the prosecution was asked? We are going all the way to Walt Disney World.

My first presupposition is that the clash between science and religion, reason and revelation, history and faith, or secularism and fundamentalism is not the dominant background against which to imagine Christianity's future. Of course it was necessary for science to break the power of religion over matters beyond its competence and of course there will always be residual skirmishes between them. But often, all too often, past (and, for some people, still present) debates involved misunderstandings of the literary protocols, cultural presumptions, and historical situations of those inaugural Christian texts, claims, titles, and beliefs which *both* sides took for granted.

The village atheist or secularist said this: Virginal conceptions, divine births, supernatural miracles, resurrected bodies, and heavenly ascensions never did, never could, never will take place in human history. The pious pastor or fundamentalist said: True, they do not happen regularly or normally, but they all happened once long ago to our Jesus. General impossibility dueled with special uniqueness but nobody insisted: wait, before you believe or disbelieve, how do you know what those ancient writers wanted to say to you? You read Aesop and do not rush to belief or disbelief. You do not say: did you know that, by the power of Zeus, animals could speak in ancient Greece? Or, did you know that one ancient Greek named Aesop believed they could? How do you judge what ancient writers wanted to communicate and must you not do that before deciding whether you believe them or not?

Listen, for example, to an early Christian apologist and an equally early pagan polemicist arguing over those Christian stories and note this base-feature of their debate. Nobody claims either uniqueness or impossibility against the other. The pro-Christian defender Justin Martyr, writing his *First Apology* in the middle of the second century, and the anti-Christian attacker Celsus, writing his *On the True [Pagan] Doctrine* about twenty-five years later, had to agree on this base-point. Virginal conception and divine impregnation at the start of a life or risen apparition and heavenly ascension at the end of a life were accepted possibilities of their cultural environment. Neither writer claimed that such events could not happen. Neither writer claimed that such events were unique. This is Justin's somewhat stunning assertion in his *First Apology* 21–22:[1]

> And when we say also that the Word, who is the first-birth of God, was produced without sexual union, and that He, Jesus Christ, our Teacher, was crucified and died, and rose again, and ascended into heaven, we propound nothing different from what you believe regarding those whom you esteem sons of Jupiter. For you know how many sons your esteemed writers ascribed to Jupiter: Mercury . . . Aesculapius . . . Bacchus . . . Hercules . . . the sons of Leda, and Dioscuri . . . Perseus . . . Bellerophon . . . Ariadne . . .

And what of the emperors who die among yourselves, whom you deem worthy of deification, and in whose behalf you produce some one who swears he has seen the burning Caesar rise to heaven from the funeral pyre? . . . But if any one objects that He was crucified, in this also He is on a par with those reputed sons of Jupiter of yours, who suffered . . . For their sufferings at death are recorded to have been not all alike, but diverse; so that not even by the peculiarity of His sufferings does He seem to be inferior to them; but, on the contrary, as we promised in the preceding part of this discourse, we will now prove Him superior — or rather have already proved Him to be so — for the superior is revealed by His actions . . . And in that we say that He made whole the lame, the paralytic, and those born blind, we seem to say what is very similar to the deeds said to have been done by Aesculapius.

Justin argues quite clearly that Jesus is better than all those other divine incarnations because "the superior is revealed by His actions." Still the argument could not be, in pro-Christian apologetics, that the case of Jesus was unique nor, in anti-Christian polemics, that such an event could not happen. Here, for example, is the best that Celsus can do to refute Christian claims about Jesus' divine conception and bodily resurrection in his work *On the True [Pagan] Doctrine*: [2]

Are we to think that the high God would have fallen in love with a woman of no breeding? . . . After all, the old myths of the Greeks that attribute a divine birth to Perseus, Amphion, Aeacus and Minos are equally good evidence of their wondrous works on behalf of mankind — and are certainly no less lacking in plausibility than the stories of your followers. What have you done [Jesus] by word or deed that is quite so wonderful as those heroes of old? . . . Has there ever been such an incompetent planner: When he was in the body, he was disbelieved but preached to everyone; after his resurrection, apparently wanting to establish a strong faith, he chooses to show himself to one woman and a few comrades only. When he was punished, everyone saw; yet risen from the tomb, almost no one.

Apart from sneers and put-downs, Celsus' core-argument is about the inferiority of Jesus: "What have you done [Jesus] by word or deed that is quite so wonderful as those heroes of old?" The debate is about competing divine incarnations in a world where divine incarnation is assumed as regularly possible. Our reading of such texts must, therefore, either remove *all* or retain *all* such divine incarnations and, either way, the choice still stands, for example, (the ascension of) Jesus Christ *or* (the ascension of) Julius Caesar? Which side are you on? In other words, where do you find the ultimate meaning of life more adequately exemplified and embodied? In imperial power or in peasant justice? We used to think that the ancients believed dumb stuff, told silly stories, and that, at the Enlightenment, we got smart and ceased to believe them. I think it more accurate to say that the ancients told powerful parables and that, at the Enlightenment, we were dumb enough to take them all literally.

A Modest Disposal

Every year now the Southern Baptist Convention locks horns (possibly an unfortunate metaphor) with Walt Disney Incorporated. The debate is not over morality or even over differing views of morality. It is not over the Bible or even over differing views of where it is permanently valid (love your enemies) and where it is socially relative (slaves obey your masters). It is actually over the global control of fantasy. The contest is between two giant corporations over the worldwide missionary expansion of illusional entertainment. Both are, at least in large doses, equally if differently dangerous. With Walt Disney Incorporated it is sometimes difficult to tell reality from fantasy as cartoon characters, literary figures, historical events, geographical places, and eventually religious traditions disappear into animated illusion. With the Southern Baptist Convention it is sometimes difficult to distinguish between Christian love and social hate (soft hate, maybe?) as their opposition so often supports, enflames, and feeds lethal actions surely outside their intention but not thereby outside their responsibility. But, locked together, the battle-object is obvious. Who, for the next century or even the next millennium, will control the transmutation of reality into fantasy, of religious reality into religious fantasy and of secular reality into secular fantasy?

My present hope is that Walt Disney Incorporated and the Southern Baptist Convention amalgamate freely and evenly, not a hostile takeover nor even a friendly buy-out of one by the other but an absolutely equal combination, maybe like Harper and Collins became HarperCollins*Publishers*. They could become the BaptistDisney*Entertainments*. Impossible? Maybe. But just think about it. A new giant theme park, wiping out any recent gains made by Universal Studios' Escape, and taking up all the rest of Central Florida, from sea to shining sea. It could have an interactive Garden of Eden where visitors could create different original sins and divergent histories of the world or an interactive Rapture Ride and Millennial Slaughter where visitors could invent alternative atrocities to exterminate the ungodly. The possibilities are unlimited.

I can see only one cloud on that horizon. The United States Justice Department might move in to prevent a monopoly on world fantasy. But a good legal defense should be able to win that one. There are still other major contenders in the market. There are Hollywood's special-effects wizards, England's Royal Family (I sympathize with the Queen's admission that she'd had an "anus horribilis," presumably referring to Charles, in her Windsor Castle speech), Rome's Vatican City, and Israel's National Parks Authority which, according to Time magazine for February 22, 1999, "has approved a 262 ft.-long transparent bridge to be built just below the surface of the Sea of Galilee so visitors can follow in the footsteps of Christ. . . . After it opens in August, [the contractor Ron Major] expects up to 800,000 people a year to pay a minimum fee to walk on water. And, yes, lifeguards will be on hand in case anyone strays from the true path." With such competition in place, BaptistDisney*Entertainments* would not have a monopoly on global fantasy, just a Number 1 ranking among its proponents.

The gains and losses of the Enlightenment Era are already clear and set, although, of course, there will still be legal disputes well into the next century. But my second presupposition is that the Entertainment Era is the future's immediate background and that the dominant clash will now be between fantasy and religion. What I am trying to imagine, then, is what Christianity must do clearly and honestly to distinguish itself from fantasy. If it does not do that, it will certainly survive but as an important and even lucrative subdivision of world-wide entertainment and global illusion. I am also very aware that Yeats said somewhere that a heart grown up on fantasy, grows old on brutality.

The Christian Trinity in the Future

There is also a special presupposition for this specific section. I consider religion to be an inalienable part of our humanity. It is not a simple and out-dated projection of fear or hope but a permanent and necessary interaction with the mystery that surrounds us. I think of that more as a working hypothesis than an act of faith because it is born of a basic trust in religion's presence across most of time and space as well as a basic distrust of those who said we could do without it but then either displaced it with the ultimacy of unreligion or replaced it with the bottom-line of materialism. None of that ignores or excuses the evils done in religion's name. Such evils are done in the name of everything profoundly human: sex and love, marriage and family, nation and state, organization and institution. Religion, for me, is like language. We are not hard-wired for this one or that one but we are hard-wired for the process itself.

I spent twenty-six years teaching required general education classes to undergraduates at DePaul University in Chicago. In those years I spent far more time with comparative religion courses than with New Testament or historical Jesus ones. How does Christian belief in the Trinity, in God-as-Triune, stand within comparative religion and how will it stand for the future? I do not take immediate refuge in mystery because, in this case, the mystery seems a little like divine multiple-personality disorder or transcendental dysfunctional-family syndrome. There must be something fundamentally and even universally true about that Trinity-God even if that Christian terminology of persons and natures was simply its once-upon-a-time Greek clothing. But what is that permanently valid insight that we must retain for the future?

It does not seem adequate to respond that the Christian God appears to us as Creator, Redeemer, and Consoler, for example, since that makes the threeness rather relative. It could be two, three, or more, so that those three were but some of the presumably far more multiple faces or masks of divinity, the divergent ways in which it appeared and was named by us. Yet the trinitarian or triadic structure of the Christian God did not seem to be as indeterminate as that. It was inviolable internally and externally as three, no more, no less.

My proposal is that Trinity is not just the special or peculiar nature of the Christian God. It is the very structure of the Holy, the Divine, the Transcendent. I do not speak about the structure of the

Holy *in itself*. That is not any sort of special protection for divinity but simply because in-itself-ness is always beyond us, even about ourselves to ourselves. But I speak about the structure of the Holy as seen by every religion I know and any religion I can imagine. Here, then, is how I understand the Holy as Trinity, the triadic and interactive loop of the Sacred as perceived by humans across the vast diversity of world religions. Here is how I imagine a future for the Christian Trinity. That triadic structure is metaphoricity, locality, and particularity.

Metaphoricity. There is, first of all, metaphoricity. Metaphor is seeing-*as*, seeing the clouds *as* ships, the sky *as* sea, and then saying that the clouds *sailed* across the sky. The Holy, the ultimate referent of religion, is always approached through some base-metaphor, some absolutely fundamental seeing-as. Metaphoricity is intractably necessary as an inevitable first moment in human relationship with the divine. We do not just name it, we invoke it *as*-this or *as*-that. I see clearly four major symbols or base-metaphors which religion has produced. There are probably others but these are the ones I see most obviously. The Holy is imagined as power, order, state, or person. By *power* I mean something like birth or storm, for example, the Holy in most oral or primordial religions. By *order* I mean something like our road-traffic or air-control systems but neither created nor controlled by us, nor, indeed, by any transcendent agent. It is simply there as the pattern of the universe, for example, the Holy as mandate of heaven in Confucianism. By *state* I mean something like peace or happiness but not under human control or manipulation, for example, the Holy as Nirvana in Buddhism. By *person(s)* I mean Supreme Being(s), person(s) like us but infinitely superior, endowed not so much with hands or feet, sex or gender, as with infinite intelligence and omnipotent will. And here the word God is entirely appropriate for it means precisely this, the Holy as person(s). In Christianity, for example, that metaphoricity is very deeply invested, first as person, next, as parent, and finally as father. But all of those fundamental metaphors speak truthfully about the Holy, each of them creates different social superstructures and cultural communities with benefits and liabilities from that base-metaphor's content, none of them is totally and exclusively correct, and all of them together are far more accurate than any one of them alone.

Locality. That first structural component, metaphoricity, always leads directly into a second one I term locality or manifestation. There is always some material phenomenon in which that metaphoricity is especially, particularly, or uniquely made evident on earth. It can be almost anything although, in every case, the metaphor's locality seems spatially, ecologically, historically, or culturally ineluctable. It can be some person, place, or thing, some individual or collectivity, some cave or shrine or temple, some clearing in the forest or tree in the desert where that ultimate referent is peculiarly met or specially experienced. In Christianity, for example, that locality is Jesus in whose vision and program, life and death, vindication and resurrection the justice of the Holy is uniquely known.

Particularity. Both metaphoricity and locality are always something experienced and accepted by believers but not by nonbelievers. This mystery of particularity closes the trinitarian loop and here the best analogy to divine faith is human love. You must experience faith or love as if it could not be other but, simultaneously, you must also acknowledge that of course it could be other. Imagine this. I wake up tomorrow morning next to my wife Sarah and say, "If I had not met you, fallen in love with you, and married you, I would probably have met someone else, fallen in love with her, married her, and be waking up next to her this morning." That would be a very imprudent way to start my day, yet it is probably true. It is also unspeakably crude in its denial of human particularity. Or imagine this. A young couple have just lost their first-born child and I tell them, "Don't worry, you can always have another one." That, too, is unspeakably cruel in its denial of human particularity. So also, then, with your religion, you must experience it as if no alternative were even possible. But out of the corner of your mind, you must also recognize that alternatives are always present. Particularity is not relativity, not the belief that anything goes or that everything is the same, but the acceptance that our humanity, at its deepest moments and profoundest depths, is individual and specific.

For individuals, groups, and communities this metaphoricity and that locality, this seeing-as and that seeing-where, seem absolutely true and all other possibilities but heresy, apostasy, infidelity, mistake at best and treason at worst. Whether through genetic or ethnic occasions, personal or cultural drives, psychological or social forces, *this* metaphoricity and *this* locality are experienced as choosing us rather than we just choosing them. I do not say (although I know it is true): I might have been a Muslim or a Hindu but I was born in Ireland and so I'm a Christian Roman Catholic.

Particularity, too, is part of the structure of the Holy and it is only through it that *Metaphoricity* and *Locality* act upon us.

My understanding is that every religion works within that triadic loop of metaphoricity, locality, and particularity. So also must Christianity not because it is Christian but because it is religion. But how that structure has been invested and must continue to be invested in the future is much more open for discussion. If there is any validity to that trinitarian structure of the Holy, not in itself I repeat, but as interactively perceived rather than simply projected by religion itself, the following are possible questions for the future. First: how will Father, Son, and Holy Spirit be understood against that background? Second: what is the metaphor of those metaphors, the metametaphor or megametaphor for person, state, order, power? Third: since we are moral beings, will that metametaphor have to be moral? For example, whether we imagine the Holy as power, order, state, or person, are those metaphors moral ones and, if so, how so?

The Historical Jesus in the Future

For this present seminar, I will not repeat my general reconstruction of the historical Jesus and/or earliest (that is, pre-Pauline) Christianity. I presume you all have had the good taste to read *The Birth of Christianity* or, if not, will immediately remedy that sad situation. You know that for almost thirty years I have argued in print that Jesus' Kingdom of God was eschatological but not apocalyptic (for example, *In Parables*, pp. 25–26, in 1973). By *eschatological* I mean any vision or program for which this world is so radically unjust that only transcendent remedy is possible. By *apocalyptic* I mean that type of eschatology that awaits an imminent divine intervention to eradicate injustice and violence here below and *to establish a utopian world of justice and peace on earth*. I think, and continue to think, that, first, apocalyptic is one, and only one form of eschatology, and that, second, Jesus invoked another form which I termed ethical eschatology, namely, a radical resistance to systemic injustice and structural *dys*tribution (may I create that word?) which embodies for him, his companions, and anyone living accordingly, the immediate presence of the Kingdom of God on earth.

I confess for myself, by the way, that falling stars, laborless fertility, and the panoply of most apocalyptic scenarios are far easier to imagine or expect than to imagine, let alone expect, a non-violent world (or a non-violent God). That absolutely staggers my imagination. I also confess that *sustained* and non-violent resistance to the cosmic normalcy of structural injustice strikes me as impossible without transcendental sources for such conviction, courage, and continuance.

Be all that as it may, I wonder about two points as the (majority?) apocalyptic interpretation of the historical Jesus and the (minority?) counter-interpretation of a non-apocalyptic one harden into fixed positions. One point is that the counter-arguments for non-apocalyptic may remain more negative than positive and, trapped in that very negativity, the agenda may be set by their opponents. Another is more complex and has to do with public discourse, with the likelihood of misunderstanding us within popular culture. What do most people hear when scholars argue whether Jesus expected the imminent end of the world — or not? What do they get from a word like apocalyptic or non-apocalyptic? Against a background of *Armageddon*, *Deep Impact*, or *End of Days* what do ordinary people understand about biblical apocalyptic? In that context, and looking to a future beyond the year 2000, I want to insist here, not on a non-apocalyptic versus an apocalyptic Jesus but on four distinctions which an apocalyptic Jesus (*if* he were such) and apocalyptic Christians (*those* which were such) would have presumed in that first-century Jewish context. It must always be remembered, by the way, that however you understand apocalyptic will profoundly effect how you understand resurrection since resurrection is an inseparable part of apocalyptic expectation or announcement.

A First Distinction: Destructive or Transformative Apocalypse

This is a crucial and foundational distinction between divine destruction of the material earth (creation repealed) and divine transformation of the unjust world (evil repulsed). It is one, I think, on which all biblical scholars would agree. Biblical apocalypticists wanted only the latter event and, even if the former is ever envisaged, it is only as a subordinate part or necessary concomitant to that latter event. In any case, it is that latter event which is primarily or exclusively in focus. Their emphasis is on utopian transformation and not on global destruction. They imagined a divinely established utopia of fertility and prosperity, justice and peace, equality and serenity. Cosmic catastrophe or material cataclysm, no matter how terrible or total, is not the same as apocalyptic consummation. It is, I think, necessary to emphasize this both in current scholarship and in contemporary popularization much more now than ever before. I do not think that we scholars, even or especially in our debates on an apocalyptic versus a non-apocalyptic Jesus, have insisted enough on that fundamental distinction between an ending of material earth and an ending of human injustice, between the amorality and secularity of current apocalypticism and the morality and divinity of ancient apocalypticism.

A Second Distinction: Material or Social Apocalypse

I want to bracket the argument over whether apocalyptic language is to be taken literally and not metaphorically lest that lead us into another impasse (yes it is! *vs.* no it is not!). But two asides before continuing. One: was Virgil being literal with an imminent golden age not needing dye-works as lambs would be born already hued to purple, saffron, and scarlet? Two: even if that is metaphorical, one must still ask metaphorical of *what*? Is it of imperial peace established by the Roman God of power or of cosmic equality established by the Jewish God of justice?

Whether the language is literal or metaphorical, what about *priorities* within it? I am avoiding a division in apocalyptic language between what is literal and what is metaphorical by asking a different question: within that language, what is necessary, unnegotiable, and essential; what is unnecessary, negotiable, and unessential? Imagine the standard consummations of Jewish and/or Christian apocalypses as divided into three moments, effects, phenomena, or events:

- Event A: Peoples (vengeance and/or justice established, universal peace, total equality, etc.)
- Event B: Lands (abundant fertility, unlabored husbandry, all animals domesticated, etc.)
- Event C: Heavens (darkened sun, lightless moon, star falling, etc.)

Even if apocalypticists thought of them as one undifferentiated package, what would they say if confronted with this choice? You can have the social Peoples-Event without the material Lands&Heavens-Events or you can have the material Lands&Heavens-Events without the social Peoples-Event? They would surely have opted for the Peoples-Event above all others and that has to do with priority of Peoples even if not the metaphoricity of Lands&Heavens. They wanted the Peoples-Event but could only imagine it within a totality of Peoples&Lands&Heavens-Event. Total apocalypse is all those social and material elements together. Social apocalypse is a priority within that totality.

For a specific example, consider a Jewish apocalypse in *Sibylline Oracles* 2, dated to the time of Augustus, a decade or so before or after the turn of the eras. The Heavens-Event is certainly there: "the heavenly luminaries will crash together" and "all the stars will fall together from heaven on the sea" (2:200–202). The Lands-Event is also there in "life without care," in "three springs of wine, honey, and milk," in an earth that "will then bear more abundant fruits spontaneously," and in a world with "no spring, no summer, no winter, no autumn" (2:316, 318, 321–322, 328). But so also is the Peoples-Event. After the punishment of the unjust, this is the reward of those who "were concerned with justice and noble deeds" (2:319–320, 321–324):

> The earth will belong equally to all, undivided by walls or fences. . . . Lives will be in common and wealth will have no division. For there will be no poor man there, no rich, and no tyrant, no slave. Further, no one will be either great or small anymore. No kings, no leaders. All will be on a par together.

John Collins, whose translation from the *Old Testament Pseudepigrapha* (vol. 1, pp. 350–53) I am gratefully using, notes that "most scholars incline to the opinion that such passages were taken over as part of the Jewish original" into their later Christian adaptation and usage (vol. 1, p. 330). Here is how that apocalyptic vision concludes (vol. 1, pp. 330–35):

> To these pious ones imperishable God, the universal ruler, will also give another thing. Whenever they ask the imperishable God to save men from the raging fire and deathless gnashing he will grant it, and he will do this.

> For he will pick them out again from the undying fire
> and set them elsewhere and send them on account of his own
> people . . .

Collins footnotes that one manuscript-family inserted a refutation of that gracious conclusion and blamed Origen for making a similar suggestion: "Plainly false. For the fire which tortures the condemned will never cease. Even I would pray that this be so, though I am marked with very great scars of faults, which have need of very great mercy. But let babbling Origen be ashamed of saying that there is a limit to punishment" (1.353, n. c3). A Christian scribe rejects the Jewish original.

My question is again about priority, not metaphoricity. Why did anyone want, for example, that celestial inversion-effect in which the unusual arrival of darkness replaced the usual normalcy of light unless it was accompanied by a terrestrial inversion-effect in which the unusual arrival of justice replaced the usual normalcy of injustice? Granted, for here and now, that one is neither metaphorical nor metonymical of the other, what about priorities within that double inversion? On the one hand, would it be apocalyptically adequate to get justice without darkness? On the other, would it be apocalyptically adequate to get darkness without justice? If apocalypticists could not have both, which would they have chosen? What, if one had to choose, was essential, what unessential? What if ancients (or moderns?) had to make this choice? Which do you want: the no-fences world without the no-stars or the no-stars without the no-fences world? Which do you want: the all-on-a-par world without the abundant-fruits-spontaneously or the abundant-fruits-spontaneously without the all-on-a-par world? Granted they might like it all as a total package deal, and absent any metaphoricity, were all apocalyptic details on the same level of importance or were there clear priorities in everyone's mind?

A Third Distinction:
Negative or Positive Apocalypse

I take this distinction very gratefully from another scholar but she should not be held responsible for my present usage. Paula Fredriksen asked this question: "The twelve tribes are restored, the people gathered back to the Land, the Temple and Jerusalem are renewed and made splendid, the Davidic monarch restored: God's Kingdom is established. What place, if any, do Gentiles have in such a kingdom?" She responds: "We can cluster the material around two poles. At the negative extreme, the nations are destroyed, defeated, or in some way subjected to Israel . . . At the positive extreme, the nations participate in Israel's redemption. The nations will stream to Jerusalem and worship the God of Jacob together with Israel" (pp. 544–545). Both results are present side-by-side in Micah, for example. The negative pole is in 5:15 as God warns that, "in anger and wrath I will execute vengeance on the nations that did not obey." The positive pole is in 4:1–4. "In days to come the mountain of the Lord's house shall be established as the highest of the mountains, and shall be raised up above the hills. Peoples shall stream to it, and many nations shall come and say: 'Come, let us go up to the mountain of the Lord, to the house of the God of Jacob; that he may teach us his ways and that we may walk in his paths.' For out of Zion shall go forth instruction, and the word of the Lord from Jerusalem. He shall judge between many peoples, and shall arbitrate between strong nations far away; they shall beat their swords into plowshares, and their spears into pruning hooks; nation shall not lift up sword against nation, neither shall they learn war any more; but they shall all sit under their own vines and under their own fig trees, and no one shall make them afraid; for the mouth of the Lord of hosts has spoken."

First, Gentiles are not exterminated because they are Gentiles but because Gentiles had increasingly oppressed Israel ever since she became a colony of successive imperial conquerors. And, second, they are not converted to become ethnically Jews but, while remaining Gentiles (for example, males would not be circumcised), they are converted to the justice and righteousness, morality and ethics of the Jewish God. I agree with Fredriksen on that last point. "Eschatological Gentiles ... those who would gain admission to the Kingdom once it was established, would enter as Gentiles. They would worship and eat together with Israel, in Jerusalem, at the Temple. The God they worship, the God if Israel, will have redeemed them from the error of idolatry: he will have saved them—to phrase this in slightly different idiom—graciously, apart from the works of the Law" (p. 548).

That choice between, in Fredriksen's terms, negative or positive extremes, is also, in my terms, the choice between human extermination or human conversion, between divine vengeance or divine justice and, ultimately, between transcendental violence or transcendental non-violence. It is a question whether God's final solution of evil is the genocidal slaughter of all evil-doers. It is a question about transcendental eth(n)ic cleansing. It is a question for both Jews and Christians. It is a much more important question, in a way, than whether Jesus was apocalyptic or non-apocalyptic. It is a question about the character of the God into whose Kingdom we are invited to enter.

A Fourth Distinction:
Primary or Secondary Apocalypse

This distinction occurred to me in thinking about an article by John Kloppenborg but he should not be held responsible for my reformulation and may not even agree with its content. He distinguished between *apocalyptic* eschatology and what he termed *symbolic* eschatology. His point was that while "it is difficult to miss the pervasive eschatological tenor" of even the sapiential elements in the Q *Gospel*, "it is another question whether the term apocalyptic is an accurate characterization for the redeployment of these wisdom materials"(p. 291). In other words "it is important to ask whether the presence of an eschatological horizon justifies the label 'apocalyptic'" (p. 292). He concluded that the Q *Gospel* used apocalyptic language "creatively to dramatize the transfiguration of the present: apocalyptic symbols lend their force both negatively, by the subverting of confidence in the everydayness of existence, and positively, by buttressing a vision of rich and empowered existence based on the instruction of Jesus" (p. 304). That instruction (better, for me, that lifestyle) was "Q's advocacy of an ethic characterized by non-violence (Q 6:27–28), refusal to participate in normative means of preserving honor through resort to courts or to retaliation (Q 6:29), and the idealization of poverty (6:20b; 12:33–34; 16:13), detachment (14:26–27), and homelessness (9:57–58; 10:4–10)" (p. 305).

I rephrase and generalize Kloppenborg's distinction as follows, with appropriate apologies to its author. *Primary* apocalypticism demands immediate actions or extraordinary ethics because of the expectation of imminent consummation. You must give everything away, cease all family relations, retire to the desert, and wait in prayer and fasting for the coming end. The ethical slogan, in other words, is *interim* as one proposes an in-the-meanwhile ethics or a special waiting-for-the-end ethics and those ethics may be sensible only as such. Maybe they might survive being wrong (one might have learned to like the desert) but their future, granted failure, is very precarious. *Secondary* apocalypticism demands immediate actions or extraordinary ethics because of the permanent character and abiding revelation of God. This is how one should be living and what one should be doing here and now in any case and apocalyptic imminence is sanction rather than cause. This is what God demands and you better pay attention because the end is near. That is what Kloppenborg sees in the *Q Gospel*. I too see it there and also in the Didache. I think that Did. 16, whether imminent or distant, whether always expected or quietly postponed, is the sanction rather than the basis for Did. 1–15. The failure of Did. 16 to happen will not necessarily destroy that community because its truth is experienced in the success of its lifestyle in imitation of the *tropoi* (ways) of the Lord (Jesus/God). The ethical slogan there is *semper interim*, the meanwhile is always.

Compare, as conclusion, the following two general admonitions and focus, for example, on their divergent advice about an unmarried virgin woman. First, as an example of primary apocalypticism, think of Paul's advice (not demand) about marriage in 1 Corinthians 7, an advice perfectly reasonable in terms of the approaching end. Celibacy is better, wiser, more appropriate: "I wish that all were as I myself am. . . . I think that, in view of the impending crisis, it is well for you [virgins] to remain as you are. . . . the appointed time has grown short; from now on, let even those who have wives be as though they had none . . . and those who deal with the world as though they had no dealings with it. For the present form of this world is passing away" (7:7, 26, 29, 31). Second, as a counter-example of secondary apocalypticism, think about this demand (not advice) from the *Damascus Document*: CD-A, col. XIV: "And this is the rule of the Many, to provide for all their needs: the salary of two days each month at least. They shall place it in the hand of the Inspector and of the judges. From it they shall give to the orphans and with it they shall strengthen the hand of the needy and the poor, and to the elder who [is dy]ing, and to the vagabond, and to the prisoner of a foreign people, and to the girl who has no protector, and to the unma[rried woman] who has no suitor; and for all the works of the company, and [the house of the company shall not be deprived of its means]"[3].

In terms of imminent expectation both these authors were incorrect. Paul's advice, although gently given, would have to be reviewed in terms of that failure of imminent apocalypse. The *Damascus Document's* advice was not derived from nor dependent upon that imminence although it may have been rendered more urgent by its expectation. In any case, the latter's ethical imperative stands as valid, no matter what happens.

Four Distinctions and Future Debates

These, then, are my suggestions for the future. First, we should clarify as publicly and honestly as we can, the meaning of words like eschatological or non-eschatological, apocalyptic or non-apocalyptic, and, thereafter, we should make certain we are positively clear in what we uphold and not just negatively clear in what we oppose. Second, we should insist that those claiming an apocalyptic Jesus and/or earliest Christianity locate them on each side of those four distinctions: destructive or transformative, material or social, negative or positive, primary or secondary (and are there other ones?). I think, but we shall see what happens, that apocalyptic reconstructionists would have to opt for transformative, social, positive, and secondary apocalyptic in order to make sense of their evidence. In any case, I do not want the apocalyptic and majority opinion (I think it is that now) to avoid those questions by being allowed to insist on "apocalyptic" against "non-apocalyptic" as fixed and unpacked positions.

The Christian Church in the Future

That title "Christian Church" allows me to ignore the inconvenient fact of Christian multiplicity, not just the perfectly legitimate realities of local and regional, historical and theological, cultural and liturgical practice, but the illegitimate reality best expressed as "See how these Christians hate one another." I ignore it to ask this question: Is Christianity like sex or like politics?

If we are asked why we come together to worship, come together at church, we might answer that we are social beings and that we must conduct important human affairs as corporate and combined rather than as individual and isolated operations. Of course. We have all sorts of things that people do together, all sorts of clubs, groups, meetings, organizations, but most of those activities are also conducted quite independently as well. If you have a boat, for example, you can mind your own business and sail alone or you can, if you want, join a boating club. You can, but you do not have to do so.

Back to my initial question: Is Christianity like sex or like politics? Sex, love, and marriage are profoundly human and holy, but we usually do not come together at certain times and places to conduct those activities in common unison and all together. Christianity could be like that. We could worship God through Christ in the privacy of our own homes. Like we have a bathroom or a bedroom, we could even have a Godroom. We could all know that everyone else does something more or less the same and that religious traditions are passed down, continued, and honored as part of family heritage. Why is Christianity, or any other religion, not like that? Why do we hint or insist that there is something fundamentally corporate about it, something far more profoundly corporate than the usual proclivity to clubbing and grouping in any other human activity?

Think for a moment about politics, and I speak about American politics as a resident alien who does not get to vote and elect but certainly gets to watch and wonder. Despite America's roaring individualism, it does not have dozens of splinter parties, it does not even have, so far, a small independent party with enough seats to play off the two big parties against one another in Congress. Politics, apparently, is serious business, at least for getting what politicians want if not for getting what the country needs. Be that as it may, it *is* serious business and for that you organize. You organize, not just for club-companionship but for getting something done. Irrespective of what that something is, and be it good or bad, you organize for effective action.

When I compare American Christianity and American politics, then, one difference is clear. Politics is serious about action, Christianity is not. The historical Jesus, however, talked about the Kingdom of God, not the Community of God or even the Church of God. That word was clearly adversative in its early first-century context, was clearly 100% religious and 100% political, was clearly a deliberate challenge to the Kingdom of Caesar. Because of that, the Kingdom movement had both a vision and a program, and it was for action rather than talk that Jesus died on a Roman cross. Apart from conspiracy, the Romans did not waste that ultimate execution on philosophers or sages. Similarly with Paul. He did not settle down and run a parish at Corinth or Ephesus. He knew that the *Ecclesia* was taking on the *Imperium* and that only empire-wide organization could effectively begin such an assault. The Kingdom and the Ecclesia were to establish, from the bottom upwards, that utopian vision of the distributive and systemic justice of the Jewish God over against the normalcy of human greed and imperial violence that was, from the top downwards, the Roman Empire. That is still the same and only destiny of the Christian Church, that is still the same and only reason for which it needs institution, that is still the same and only reason for which it needs organization.

Once again, I conclude with some suggestions for the future. But first an admission. I do not celebrate, as some of my colleagues do, the idea of a second Reformation because I consider the first one basically a disaster. Of course, there were reformations of Roman Catholicism badly needed, long overdue, and still awaiting completion. But what we got from those past centuries was this disjunction: a Roman Catholicism that lacked any internal criticism, any loyal opposition, any process for necessary change that could not be controlled or coopted; a Protestantism, that with nothing to protest against, splintered itself into ever more minute and irrelevant churches and sects. A plague, maybe, on both your houses?

My suggestions are these. First, that somewhat imaginary "Christian Church" may need to decide whether its God is more concerned with distributive rather than retributive justice, that is, with the fair and equitable allocation of the material bases of life (like land in the Old Testament, food in the New Testament, etc., etc.). Second, it may also need to decide whether that God's retributive justice is always built internally and organically into *dy*stributive (in)justice (I like that new word) rather than being externally and judicially appended at some future consummation. Third, and consequent in those preceding decisions, it may finally need to decide whether its own destiny is primarily or even exclusively concerned with individual and personal injustice or with structural and systemic justice here below. Finally, it may want to distinguish clearly between Christianity and chloroform, baptism and lobotomy, worship and Prozac.

Notes

1. Roberts, *The Ante-Nicene Fathers,* vol. 1, pp. 316–18.
2. Hoffman, *Celsus,* pp. 57–58, 59, 68.
3. García Martínez, *Dead Sea Scrolls,* p. 44.

Works Consulted

Crossan, John Dominic, *In Parables.* San Francisco, CA: Harper & Row, 1973.

Fredriksen, Paula, "Judaism, The Circumcision of Gentiles, and Apocalyptic Hope: Another Look at Galatians 1 and 2," *Journal of Theological Studies,* 42 (1991), 532–64.

Hoffman, R. Joseph (Trans.), *Celsus: On the True Doctrine.* New York: Oxford University Press, 1987.

Kloppenborg, John S., "Symbolic Eschatology and the Apocalypticism of Q." *Harvard Theological Review 80 (1987), 287–306.*

García Martínez, Florentino, *The Dead Sea Scrolls Translated. The Qumran Texts in English.* Trans. Wilfred G. E. Watson. 2nd ed. [¹1994]. Brill: Leiden & Grand Rapids, MI: Eerdmans. 1996.

Roberts, Alexander, James Donaldson, and A. Cleveland Coxe, *The Ante-Nicene Fathers.* 10 vols. American Reprint of the Edinburgh Edition. New York: Scribner's, 1926.

Wright, Nicholas Thomas, *Jesus and the Victory of God.* Vol. 2 of *Christian Origins and the Question of God.* Minneapolis: Fortress Press, 1997.

Lloyd Geering

the Legacy of Christianity

What is the relationship between Christianity and the post-Christian global world? Let me first briefly define how I am using these terms.

By global world I mean the world into which we are currently moving as a result of globalization. This is the process by which the whole of humanity is being drawn into one global form of human existence. We humans the world over are becoming increasingly interdependent on one another. Our material standard of living is becoming dependent on one global economy, even though this is making some very rich and some very poor. Our once independent cultures are becoming increasingly influenced by each other. The previously independent races, nations and cultures are being caught up in one society, pluralistic and yet global. More than ever before we humans face a common future and for this we must create some kind of global culture.

The global world now being formed is not a Christian world, certainly not in the sense that medieval Christendom was a Christian world. But neither is it non-Christian, in the way that the pre-Christian world of Greece and Rome was. The global world as a whole has been influenced by the Christian tradition a great deal more than is usually recognized. The global world has to be described as post-Christian. While there are still very many who personally embrace the traditional Christian beliefs (though in a vast variety of forms), Christianity no longer overtly determines the public face of western societies.

The post-Christian global world is even better described as secular. By the term "secular" I do not mean non-religious but "this-worldly". It derives from *saeculum*, which means "this world" or "this age". This connotation leaves it an open question as to whether it may be religious or not. It is only when religion is focused primarily on "other-worldliness", as has long been the case in the Christian tradition, that 'secular' appeared to be anti-religious. Harvey Cox defined secularization simply as "man turning his attention away from worlds beyond and toward this world and this time" (p. 2).[1]

How does Christianity relate to this secular global world? That depends in turn on how we define Christianity. Do we mean, for example, the belief system expressed in the creeds and confessions of the church? Does Christianity consist of living a sacramental life within the authoritative institutional structure called Mother Church? Is the essence of Christianity to be found in accepting Jesus Christ as one's personal Lord and Savior? Does Christianity mean accepting uncritically a set of ancient scriptures as the written record of what is ultimately true? Or does Christianity consist simply of a set of moral values by which to live? All these, and many other definitions, have been regarded by various groups at one time or another as the essence or *sine qua non* of Christianity.

Modern historical research has made it very clear, however, that there has never been a time when all who confessed to be Christians (or followers of Jesus) shared all the same beliefs. The New Testament phrase "the faith which was once for all delivered to the saints (Jude 3)" was itself part of the developing Christian myth. Christian beliefs have changed and diversified through the centuries. Today, more than ever before, Christianity has no definable and eternal essence on which all Christians agree. It is misleading, therefore, to use the term Christianity in a way which implies that it names some objective and unchangeable thing.

Wilfred Cantwell Smith in his seminal little book, *The Meaning and End of Religion* (1964), observed that the very use of the term Christianity is not only a modern phenomenon but it is one which confuses faith (which is essentially an attitude of trust) with what he calls the Christian cumulative tradition. This latter consists of all the objective data that have been used or produced by those who have called themselves Christians. It includes, of course, the Bible, creeds, confessions, theological systems, moral codes, myths, buildings, and social institutions. The Christian cumulative tradition includes not only all the various denominations and sects into which the Christian Church of the West has become fragmented, but it includes all of Eastern Orthodoxy, the Coptic tradition of Egypt and Ethiopia and the Nestorian tradition which reached China. Moreover the cumulative tradition includes what the main body of Christians have judged to be deviant heresies and the work of the devil.

It is unnecessarily clumsy to keep using the words 'the Christian cumulative tradition' but that is what I shall always mean hereafter when I use the word Christianity. Christianity includes everything referred to by the above definitions and yet is more extensive than them all. It includes everything which can be traced back, however indirectly, to the influence of the historical figure known as Jesus of Nazareth. If we exclude any of that complex cumulative tradition we cease to be neutral historians and we are making a sectarian judgment.

Christianity is, of course, only one of many cumulative cultural traditions. Some of them are much older than Christianity. Each cumulative cultural tradition may be likened to a stream flowing through the plains of time. Sometimes it divides and sometimes it is joined by other streams. As it flows onward, it sometimes drops its sediment and it sometimes gathers new material. It has no unchangeable essence other than being a humanly created cultural stream. In the attempt to reform the Christian stream people often speak of the danger of throwing out the baby with the bathwater. That is misleading for in actual fact there is no baby. It's all bathwater!

The chief source of the Christian cumulative tradition is to be found in the cultural stream flowing from ancient Israel. But there were other sources, too rarely acknowledged. Before even the Christian era, the Jewish stream was penetrated by tributaries from Persian Zoroastrianism and Hellenism. (Much of the Zoroastrian tradition, for example, lives on *incognito* in the Jewish, Christian and Islamic streams). The enlivening influence of Jesus of Nazareth had the effect of adding such a fresh burst of vitality to the Jewish cultural stream that it caused part of it to break out of its banks and form a new stream, which we now commonly refer to as the Judeo-Christian tradition.

In New Zealand, at a former gold-mining town called Cromwell, two great rivers used to join. The deep blue rushing waters of the Clutha river were joined by the equally fast waters of the Kawarau river, made dirty many miles upstream by the sluicing for gold. For a mile or two downstream from the junction a clear line separated the blue Clutha from the muddy Kawarau until they eventually merged as one as they rushed through the Cromwell Gorge.

When the new and fast-flowing Christian stream broke out of the banks of the Jewish stream it mingled with streams from both the Greek and Roman cultural traditions, absorbing new and significant ingredients. Philosophical terms, analytical reasoning, new notions of God and of the human condition came from the Greeks. Legal and organizational strengths came from the Romans. This quickly-developing multiple stream encountered many competitors, some of which, such as the mystery religions and Manichaeism, left further deposits. Competition forced the Christian stream to define itself. Of all the streams then flowing Christianity eventually proved to be the most enduring and, as it spread and consolidated, it created Christian culture. We call it Christian because dominant within this stream were the ideas, values, myths and goals which had come to be associated with the name Jesus Christ, many of which had not actually originated with him.

In the course of two thousand years Christianity has continued to develop and change, as it has been influenced by the thoughts, feelings and personal experiences of countless generations of people. As we look back we can now discern distinctive phases in the ongoing life of the Christian stream, such as mediaeval Christendom, the Renaissance, the Protestant Reformation.

In the last four to five hundred years, Christianity has not only spread around the world geographically but, like a river fanning out into a delta, it has diversified in its forms. Its organizational manifestation is to be found in a great variety of churches, denominations, sects, associations, movements and house groups. The ideas, personal beliefs, theologies and philosophies to be found in the cultural stream of the Christian West today are even more diverse. They have manifested themselves in the Enlightenment, the rise of empirical science, the development of new technology and the emergence of the modern secular world. Each new phase in the Christian cumulative tradition has been resisted and rejected by many as being quite foreign to its Christian past. This is because, at the very center of the Christian stream there crystallized a more rigid structure, both doctrinal and organizational. This came to be regarded by most as the unchangeable essence of the stream. It was assumed this had to be preserved in its pure and pristine state.

This ossified core of doctrine and social patterns should not be identified with the stream itself. I suggest, on the contrary, that the emergence of the modern secular, global world is not only the continuation of the Christian cumulative tradition but, in many ways, is also the logical outcome of what has preceded it. In flowing out of its cultural past, the modern secular world is to be regarded not as anti-Christian (as stalwarts of orthodoxy assert) but as a new and distinctly different stage in the evolution of the Judeo-Christian stream.

To illustrate this, let me suggest an analogy between the cultural change to Judaism initiated by the influence of Jesus and the transition from classical Christendom to today's secular culture.

At the beginning of the Christian era, the Jewish tradition had no intention of giving birth to Christianity. The new Jewish sect known as "the Christians" was regarded as an heretical movement even though its key figure Jesus of Nazareth, and his chief interpreter Paul, were both Jewish to the core. For their part the Christians did not see their movement as the abandonment of the past but as its fulfilment. They interpreted Jesus as saying, "I have not come to abolish the law and the prophets but to fulfil them" (Matt 5:17). That is why they kept the Jewish scriptures as their own.

During the first six centuries of the Christian era, the cultural stream of ancient Israel eventually issued into three streams: rabbinical Judaism, Christianity and Islam. Each claimed the patriarchs and Israelite prophets as part of their own tradition. As someone has shrewdly observed, "Islam is really Judaism *transplanted* among the Arabs and Christianity is really Judaism *transformed* for the Gentiles".

On the basis of this analogy I shall now try to show how the modern secular world, with all its faults and problems, represents a new but legitimate stage in the Judeo-Christian cultural stream. The coming of global secular world does entail the end of the ossified structure known as Christian orthodoxy but, in itself, it actually constitutes the ongoing development of the Judeo-Christian stream from which it has come. I shall attempt to illustrate this by focusing on the two chief characteristics of the modern global world — globalization and secularization.

It is not difficult to show that the seeds of globalization can be found far back in the early stages of the Judeo-Christian cultural stream. It was expressed in such words as "all the nations of the earth shall bless themselves through Abraham" (Gen 18:18) and "all nations shall gather to the presence of the LORD in Jerusalem" (Jer 3:17). Of course those Israelite thinkers were still chauvinistically assuming that all the nations would desire of their own accord to come and share the spiritual inheritance given to the people of Israel. By the time of the New Testament the Pharisees even saw themselves fulfilling a divine mission to "traverse sea and land to make a single proselyte" (Matt 23:15).

At the beginning of the Christian era, however, this vision of a global human future passed from the Jews to the Christians. Judaism retreated into its own rabbinical shell, somewhat shocked by what it had brought forth. Christians then set out on their mission to go to the ends of the earth and make disciples of all nations.

Incidentally, the Judeo-Christian cultural tradition was not the only one motivated by a vision of a global world drawing all nations together. In fact it was a special potential of all the post-axial traditions. Being no longer limited by ethnic boundaries, they each had the capacity to become global. Only three achieved this mission to all humankind to any great degree: they were the Buddhist, Christian and Islamic traditions. By about the 15th century they had penetrated the whole land mass of Eurasia and divided it up among them, forming the Christian West, the Islamic Middle East and the Buddhist Orient.

However, by building ocean-going vessels, the Christian West stole a march on the other two. During the last five centuries Christianity has spread to the two Americas, the sub-Saharan Africa, Australasia and Oceania. As recently as the beginning of the twentieth century the Christian mission to the whole globe was still very vigorous. Some even believed it was nearing its completion. This is why the Christian west has largely been instrumental in promoting the current phenomenon of globalization.

It was the intention of Christianity, of course, to incorporate the whole world into Christendom, just as, long ago, the Israelite prophets assumed all the nations would flow to Jerusalem. The Christian vision of a unified world remained almost as chauvinistic as the Jewish one had been.

While it is relatively easy to show how globalization may be attributed to Christianity, it is common to assume that secularization cannot possibly be claimed as a Christian product. Christian leaders certainly never intended to promote secularization, any more than the ancient Jews intended to give birth to Christianity. Yet the fact remains that, for better or for worse, the process of secularization emerged out of the Christian West.

Most would agree that an essential factor in the emergence of secularization has been the rise of empirical science, which in turn opened the way to modern technology. It is an historical fact that modern science and technology evolved out of Western Christian culture. Was this merely an accident of history, in that empirical science might just as easily have arisen somewhere else? Or is there an intrinsic connection between the Christian cultural stream and the rise of this modern science?

C.F. von Weizsäcker, German physicist and philosopher, in his Gifford lectures on *The Relevance of Science,* claimed that the rise of modern science cannot be accounted for except against the background of the biblical doctrine of creation, coupled with the mathematical laws of nature already present in Greek thought. He said "modern science [is] a legacy of Christianity" (p. 163). Similarly the philosopher A. N. Whitehead in his *Science and the Modern World,* contended that science originated from the medieval Christian conception of God as one which combined the personal energy of Yahweh with the rationality of a Greek philosopher. "In Asia" he said, "the conceptions of God were of a being too arbitrary or too impersonal for such ideas to have much effect on instinctive habits of mind" (p. 13). The philosopher of history, Karl Jaspers, observed that Greek science was radically different from modern Western science and the reason why the Greeks failed to achieve, real, universal science was due to their lack of the spiritual motives and moral impulses which enabled later Christian mankind to create that science out of its developing culture, even though that science eventually came into conflict with Christian orthodoxy. "Peculiar to the Christian world", he said, 'and developed nowhere else in history . . . is the relentlessness of the search for truth which manifests itself in Western science. There is no denying the fact that this science with its universality . . . . its special type of unity, originated only in the West and only on Christian soil" (pp. 67–69).

Moreover, faith in one God who had not only created the world but also remained completely separate from it meant that the earth could be expected to display the rationality of its law giver Creator. Long before today's scientists invented the term "A Theory of everything", the Christian doctrine of God (formed as it was from a synthesis of Israelite and Greek thought) already provided, for practical living, a theory of everything. God was not only the first cause in bringing the world into being; it was God's laws which constituted the structure of the physical world, and it was God's will which ultimately determined all that occurred within it.

The pioneers of empirical science were all Christians who saw themselves firmly established within the Christian tradition. They were simply trying to discover those laws of nature. They, along with other leading thinkers in the Christian West, did not intentionally or even knowingly lead the way to modern secularization. Yet, step by step, they were constructing the path which brought us to it. These people were not the bishops and popes. Here is a list of some of them: Francis of Assisi, Roger Bacon, William of Occam, John Wyclif, Francis Bacon, Isaac Newton, David Strauss, Ludwig Feuerbach, Friedrich Nietzsche. They were on the Christian margins.

Take, for example, Francis of Assisi (1181–1226), hailed today as the patron saint of conservation by secular conservationists. He was the first to reverse the Christian attitude toward the world of nature from one of negative devaluation to one of positive appreciation. Furthermore, he founded the Franciscan Order out of which came such pioneers of empirical science as Roger Bacon (1214–1292) and the pioneers of modern philosophy such as William of Occam. Occam's nominalist philosophy, known as the *via moderna,* not only influenced Luther but laid the foundations of the materialist and non-realist philosophies of the nineteenth and twentieth centuries.

As Francis and his successors revalued the physical earth upwards, so the humanists of the Renaissance, such as Erasmus (1466–1536) and Pico della Mirandola (1463–1494)[1], laid the basis for a more positive evaluation of the human condition. This led in turn to the Protestant Reformation, in which the deconstruction of the "other world" began with the sudden abolition of purgatory. This was to be followed in the nineteenth century by the rejection of hell, and the disappearance of heaven in the twentieth century. Even the Pope finally conceded this year that "heaven is not a place". In other words, there is no place called heaven. All this has advanced the process of secularization, that is, the refocusing of human attention on the world of here and now.[2]

Although the change to the modern secular world appears on the face of it to be a clear rejection of beliefs which have long been central in Christianity, we find to our surprise that, in some respects, it actually brings us closer to primitive Christianity than even medieval Christianity was. The reason is that, while modern secularization came to birth in the Christian West, the seed which led to its conception is much older and is to be found in the Jewish heritage out of which Christianity sprang. When Francis of Assisi, followed by the Renaissance humanists, began to show renewed and positive interest in this-world, they were recovering something from a much earlier time in the cultural stream. Whereas classical Christianity had come to view this as a fallen world from which people needed to be saved, the Bible begins by saying "God looked at everything he had made and behold it was very good" (Gen 1:31).

Moreover, some philosophers and scientists have observed that empirical science could only have come to birth in a culture where humans felt free to experiment with the physical world because nothing in it was believed to be sacred. It was the ancient Israelites who abolished the gods of nature who prevented humans from interfering with their domain. It was the ancient Israelites who declared that humans had been given dominion over the earth by its one and only Creator. It was the ancient Israelites who desacralized the sun, moon and heavenly bodies and proclaimed that the heavens and the earth belonged to one created system.

Though the Israelites referred to the sky as the dwelling place of God, it was not for them the eternal heaven that it later became for Christians. In Old Testament times the ultimate destiny of humankind was never conceived as being anywhere else than on earth. Among all the ancient peoples the Israelites were almost alone in accepting the complete mortality of the human condition and in abandoning the once widespread hope of some sort of life beyond death.

The hope of a life in heaven, which so dominated classical Christianity, was a later development. Those living in the Jewish and early Christian periods of the cultural stream were, relatively speaking, much more this-worldly, more secular. Certainly those early Christians looked for a new world to come, but it was not a spiritual world in the sky but a physical world like this, to replace the present one. As the author of Revelation put it: "I saw a new heaven and new earth, for the first heaven and first earth had passed away."

It was only when that new world failed to arrive that something happened. Concern about the delay of the *parousia* (or return of Christ) was being expressed as early as Paul's letter to the Thessalonians. By the end of the century this must have been more pronounced. The Fourth Gospel has even been interpreted as intended in part to allay this concern by describing church life in symbolic terms as that in which Christ was already present; C. H. Dodd referred to this interpretation as "realized eschatology". In any case it was during the second and third centuries that, in compensation for the failure of the new world to arrive, their hopes for it were transferred from a physical earth to a spiritual heaven. It occurred gradually and almost unconsciously. The creative imagination of devout Christians constructed an elaborate supernatural structure of heaven, purgatory and hell. It was soon believed to possess an ontological reality of its own, though its real significance lay in its being an imaginary visualization of the meaning of life in this world. This process led to the now all-too-familiar dichotomy of heavenly/earthly, spiritual/material, supernatural/natural, otherworldly/this-worldly.

The advent of the modern secular world has been occurring in tandem with the gradual collapse of that imagined Christian superstructure. The modern secular world view with which we are now left is very different from the medieval world view and yet, in some respects, it is closer to that of the first Christians for they lived without any awareness of that medieval supernatural structure.

The modern secular world is therefore not the anti-Christian enemy it is often made out to be, but the continuation of the Judeo-Christian cultural stream. Not only is it closer to the views of the first Christians than that of the medieval Christians, but it may be seen as the ultimate manifestation of the most distinctive core of Christianity, namely its affirmation of the incarnation.

Perhaps the first person to offer a modern interpretation of the incarnation was Ludwig Feuerbach. This he did in his book *The Essence of Christianity,* where he elaborated, in stark contrast with each other, what he called the false or theological essence of Christianity and the true or anthropological essence of Christianity. He first explained the reason why it was feasible for God to become enfleshed in the human condition (a thought which Jews and Muslims find quite unacceptable) — "God was already a human God before he became an actual man" (p. 50). The very idea of "God" originated in the human mind as a set of the highest human qualities; this was then objectified, personified and projected on to the backdrop of the heavens. That is why the New Testament rightly affirms that "God is love". Unfortunately, this projection of human virtues affected humans adversely, for it resulted in the splitting of the human condition. Humans, alienated from their highest values, were left with only their negative and destructive tendencies. That, said Feuerbach, is the real meaning of the doctrine of sin, or human alienation from God. The reason why Christianity is true, Feuerbach claimed, is that it is able to restore human beings to wholeness, by reuniting them with their highest values. They no longer live a divided existence. This was achieved by the incarnation. The myth of the incarnation of "God" in human flesh reversed the earlier mythical projection. "God", as love, could once again live within the human condition. As a result of the myth of the incarnation, "God" would dwell within the human condition where God belonged. Thus the coming new world was rightly envisaged in Rev 21:3, where it says "the dwelling of god is within humanity". This meant, of course, that the mythical throne of heaven was now left empty.

Even before Feuerbach, Hegel had interpreted the death of Jesus the God-man on the cross as symbolizing the "death of God", a phrase taken up later by Nietzsche. Feuerbach, following Hegel, took the crucifixion of Jesus to symbolize in dramatic form the end of theism. To put it in the language of myth, it was the quality of love in "God" which led "God" to abandon his heavenly throne, empty himself of his other-worldliness and dwell henceforth within the human species.

This was the real meaning of the incarnation, Feuerbach asserted, and it presented humans with a challenge. Is it the mythical objective "God" who saves us and restores us to wholeness, or is it love? "It is Love," answered Feuerbach, "for God as God has not saved us but Love . . . As God has renounced himself out of love, so we, out of love, should renounce God: for if we do not sacrifice God to love, we sacrifice love to God and . . . we have the God . . . of religious fanaticism" (p. 53).

Thus Feuerbach, with a tour de force, rediscovered in the coming of the modern secular world the culmination of the very essence of Christianity. But, if he is right, why has it taken us so long to realize it?

We may answer this simply, even if somewhat simplistically, by referring to four related steps:

1. It was the failure of Jesus to return and usher in the expected new world that led Christians of the second and third centuries to engage in the mental construction of a supernatural world to take its place. (This process somewhat parallels Aaron's fashioning of the golden calf, when Moses delayed his return from the mountain top).

2. The elevation of Jesus to a supernatural throne in the heavens had the effect of virtually cancelling out the incarnation.

3. Not until the mentally constructed supernatural world had dissolved into unreality (as it has been doing over the last four hundred years) could the ultimate significance of the incarnation come to be realised.
4. The restriction of the incarnation to one human person is to miss its full significance. The process of incarnating or humanizing the mythical God applied to the whole of humankind. Paul even hinted at this when speaking of Christ as the New Adam, or symbol of the new humankind.

Someone has observed that the first Christians went out preaching the coming of the Kingdom of God but what actually arrived was the Church. Similarly we may say that in modern times Christians went out to create a global Christendom out of the nations of the world but what has actually arrived is the global secular world.

This global secular world should not be undervalued. It has brought to the fore many virtues which were either not thought of or were often suppressed in the Christendom of pre-modern times. The affirmation of basic human rights and the value of personal freedom, for example, are special features of the modern secular world. These have led to a whole series of new freedoms – democratic freedom from absolute rule (by monarchy, aristocracy or dictator), emancipation from slavery, emancipation from racism, emancipation of women, emancipation of homosexuals. (These emancipations were not chiefly led by the clergy but by people on the margins of the Christian stream.)

This does not mean that at last the Kingdom of God has come on earth. Far from it. The secular world is far from ideal and beyond criticism. It is a world in which much is going wrong. It is a world in which we have to make some very difficult choices about our own future and the future of all planetary life. What the doctrine of the incarnation tells us is that the throne of heaven is empty. We humans are on our own. We must learn to live without the divine props thought to exist in the past. The doctrine of the incarnation tells us we humans now have to play the role of God. More than in any other living species on this planet, it may be said that the self-evolving planet, if not the universe, has become conscious in us humans with all the responsibility for the future that that entails.

That is just where the work of the Jesus Seminar suddenly becomes very relevant to the world's future. It was because of the Jesus who lived 2000 years ago that out of the Jewish cultural stream there flowed the Judeo-Christian cultural stream — Christianity for short. It was because of Christianity that the modern secular world is coming into existence. The secular global world, with all its fragility, is itself the legacy of Christianity, and ultimately the legacy of Jesus of Nazareth.

If we humans now have grave problems to solve, we need to go back to our cultural roots to understand better just how we got here and who we are. I have already suggested an analogy between the emergence of Christianity out of Judaism and the emergence of the modern secular world out of Christianity. We may take this analogy further. It was not the Jewish priests and scholars who initiated Christianity; they were strongly opposed to it. Christianity came to birth on the margins of the Jewish cumulative tradition, even though Jesus was a Jew who never rejected his Jewish roots. Similarly it was not the Christian clergy who initiated secular world; they have been and still are largely opposed to it. The secular world was initiated by Christians, but Christians who were on the margins or growing edges of the Christian cumulative tradition.

The fact that the clergy and the organized churches still see the secular world as something foreign to Christianity means that it is being left without any spiritual leadership, helping it to understand the roots from which it has sprung. The more militant leaders of secular thought, for example, may be compared with the ancient Gnostic leader Marcion who wanted the Christian tradition to sever its connection altogether with its Jewish past. That was to prove a blind path. Human culture never makes a complete break with its past and, if it attempts to do so, it is taking the path to extinction.

The world is at the cross roads. What it now needs is a group of people who can give it some moral and spiritual leadership. It should have been the clergy and church leaders, for they long gave some direction to the Christian stream; but they are failing to do so because they do not adequately understand the source and nature of the secular world. The required leaders must acknowledge the importance and value of our having reached the secular stage. They need to possess some depth of understanding and academic credibility. The Jesus Seminar is well placed to be among those who meet this need. At its core is a group of scholars who are well aware that the real world is the global secular world. And going back to Jesus of Nazareth is the logical place to start since it was from him that Christianity took its origin in moving beyond the purely Jewish stream.

But it is not the Jesus who was elevated into a mythical heaven who is of relevance to us; it is Jesus the fully human person, who gave rise to the Christian cultural stream. It is the full humanity of Jesus which has been recovered in modern times by Reimarus, Strauss, Weiss, Schweitzer, Bultmann and now the Jesus Seminar. While traditional Christians have deplored the removal of the mythical Christ as a great loss, it is actually turning out to be a great gain. Even though this human Jesus is still largely hidden behind the mythical dress with which he was so quickly clothed, it is he, and not the heavenly Christ, who shared the tensions, enigmas and uncertainties that we experience concerning the present and the future. This very thought can encourage us.

It is the Jesus who could look both appreciatively and also critically at his cultural past who can inspire us as we in turn look back to a receding Christian past and forward to an unknown global future. It is Jesus the teller of stories which shocked people out of their traditional ways of thinking and behaving who can free us from the mind-sets in which we become imprisoned. The Jesus most relevant to us is he who, far from providing ready-made answers, prompted people by his tantalizing stories, to work out their own most appropriate answers to the problems of life.

Perhaps the recovery of the human Jesus of the past is the very stimulus we need today. It is the faculty of self-criticism which has enabled the Christian cultural stream to reach the secular global sea now spreading round the world. Self-criticism needs to be exercised more than ever if this cultural stream is to continue to evolve for the full benefit of humankind in a way consistent with its long-term hopes.

From this start of trying to recover the voice-prints and foot-prints of the original Jesus, the Jesus Seminar must now broaden its scope to help provide the intellectual and spiritual leadership which the secular world now needs, and which the churches are failing to give. The Jesus Seminar has discovered that the man Jesus seems to have belonged rather more to the Wisdom stream of the ancient Israelite tradition than to the priestly, the prophetic or the Davidic traditions, where Christian orthodoxy always placed him.

Modern Old Testament scholars have observed for some time that the Wisdom literature represented the deposit of Hebrew humanism. It was always on the margins of Israelite religion and hence was placed in The Writings. It showed little interest in the great themes of the Torah and the Prophets. It was more universal to the human race; it was largely secular. It is this stream which has become so relevant for the future of the human race.

As Dietrich Bonhoeffer, struggling to understand what he called "religionless Christianity", started to speak of Jesus as "the man for others", we can now legitimately speak of him as the man of wisdom. Robert Funk has said, not only that "Jesus is one of the great sages of history" but that "Jesus is also a secular sage. His parables and aphorisms all but obliterate the boundaries separating the sacred from the secular" (p. 302).

If this be so, it was Jesus the secular sage whose long-term influence did so much, even by an indirect route, to bring the modern secular world into being. The rediscovery of this secular sage can continue to shake us out of our complacency, as he did long ago. He can challenge us to think for ourselves, spur us to act in faith and then to take full responsibility for our actions. The human Jesus of the past can yet become the Jesus of the future by providing for us the model of that human wisdom which our age so desperately needs.

Notes

1. Note his *Oration on the Dignity of Man*, written when he was only twenty-four.
2. I have discussed 'why secularization came out of the west' in greater detail in *Faith's New Age* (Collins, 1980), chap. 14.

Works cited

Cox, Harvey, *The Secular City*. SCM Press, 1966.
Feuerbach, Ludwig, *The Essence of Christianity*. Harper Torchbooks, 1957.
Funk, Robert W. *Honest to Jesus*. HarperSanFrancisco, 1996.
Geering, Lloyd, *Faith's New Age*. Collins, 1980.
Jaspers, Karl, *Nietzsche and Christianity*. Henry Regnery Company, 1961.
Smith, Wilfred Cantwell, *The Meaning and End of Religion*. 1964
Weizsäcker, C. F. von, *The Relevance of Science*. Collins, 1964.
Whitehead, A. N., *Science and the Modern World*. Cambridge University Press, 1926.

Gerd Lüdemann

from Faith to Knowldedge
the Contribution of Jesus to Cosmic Awareness

A s a born again Christian I anxiously waited for the return of Jesus on the clouds of heaven, almost on an hourly basis. Faith in my savior who had suffered for my sins and who was raised from the dead constituted the center of my life. The bible was a daily source of inspiration for new insights. It contained all the necessary moral codes and, most of all, it revealed to me that the Lord had elected me and, through his bloody death, rescued me from eternal punishment. In my religious life, the image of an executioner came very often to my mind, bringing home to me the idea of a god who has to punish because he loves, who has to threaten because he wants to help and who destroys in order to build his kingdom. The saying of Jesus which I heard every Sunday during the baptism of children, still rings in my ear: "Everyone who believes and is baptized will be saved, but one who does not believe will be damned" (Mark 16:16).

Enlightened liberal Christians who wanted to help me in my religious struggles told me what my academic teachers of theology would later only repeat: You cannot understand the Bible literally. This kind of reading, they said, is inadequate because the biblical texts belong to a specific time and consequently cannot be transferred without further ado to another time and place. I had to discover that such an approach, wise as it may seem, quite often leads to the opposite of what is said in the Bible. For example, any miracle comes to be understood as the miracle of coming to faith. Or the concrete demand which Jesus directed at the rich young man to sell every belonging of his and to give it to the poor is now interpreted as the demand to accept Jesus' word. When I asked my liberal teachers whether they expected Jesus' return on the clouds of heaven, they replied, it would be too difficult to answer such a question without being misunderstood. Therefore they still owe me an answer to that question, and to my repeated questions about the resurrection of Jesus. It was not much more than waffling that I heard, and after more than twenty years of waiting, I don't want to hear more nonsense claiming that what the Bible says about the resurrection and second coming of Jesus is true, but did not or does not take place. And to let the nonsense reach its peak: most or all of these academic theologians confess the apostle's creed every Sunday though they have given up 95% of its content. In addition, they know that, given the incredible diversity of Christian symbolism, doctrine, belief, and moral practice, the term Christian has practically turned into an empty phrase. But when I openly said that for these reasons I could and would no longer be called a Christian, they, at my home University of Göttingen, in close cooperation with the official Lutheran Church, called for my immediate dismissal from the faculty of theology.

I think the present situation is confused, to say the least, and calls for a remedy. A clear decision has to be made: either I do accept the total refutation of the dogmatic system by historical criticism or, in whatever way, I make the world of the Bible my own. In the latter case I can continue to attend Sunday service with a good conscience and can participate with all of my heart in the prayers addressed to the risen lord.

For good reasons that I don't want to go into at length, the latter option is no longer available to me. Let me just remind you that Jesus rotted away and therefore did not rise. Consequently he is not someone we can speak to in prayer. The first option seems, at first sight, to be nothing but denial and therefore not very appealing. However, any scholarly denial is a positive intellectual act that prepares the way for the new. It is an act of unveiling and therefore humanizing. Our tradition gains everything if it appears without a veil. Only then does it succeed in rising from sterile church dogmatics into the fertile sphere of life which is sometimes chaotic, but in the end is shining, warm and beautiful. But we will regain vitality in our traditions only if we can get inside the minds that formulated them in order to get a close look at their experience. What do we need to be able to do just that? First, an open mind, and second, new sources from the early Christian movement which would shed light on the early Christian experience. This would give us who were raised in the normative Christian tradition a chance to look at them from a totally different perspective.

As you all know, there existed another stream of early Christianity whose members were suppressed by bishops and other functionaries of the official church. This movement may be given the name gnosticism (from the Greek, *gnosis* "knowledge"). Primary sources from among gnostic movements have been available since the spectacular discovery of the Nag Hammadi library in December of 1945. They reflect both a radical departure from dogmatics and a deep religious experience. They fulfil the wish to have available new sources from early Christianity and help us greatly to get to know the first Christians better.

Let me now sketch the totally different meaning given to the resurrection of Jesus among these gnostic groups (Gospel of Philip):

> Those who say that the lord died first and (then) rose up are in error, for he rose up first and (then) died. If one does not first attain the resurrection, will he not die? (NHC II, 3: 56, 15–19).

In this saying the author first declares the orthodox dogma of the death and resurrection of Jesus to be an error. He then simply reverses its sequence. The resurrection, he claims, has already happened. He continues: Whoever does not experience (attain) his own resurrection (in order come to know what is unchanging), will die, here and now, a spiritual death not to mention physical death. He misses the true goal of life, imperishability and stability.

A similar notion of resurrection can be found already in the New Testament. Let me only mention two examples. In 2 Tim 2:18 a pupil of Paul attacks those who claim that the resurrection has already happened. And in the gospel of John, Jesus teaches unambiguously: "Those who hear my word and believe the one who sent me, have real life and do not come up for trial. No, they have passed through death into life" (5:24). Such a statement, however, was intolerable in the orthodox church because the majority of Christians would not give up a final judgment and resurrection of the flesh. Therefore a later corrector of John's gospel made an addition to the bold statement about the eternal presence of the resurrection of believers, writing: "The time is coming when all who are in their graves will . . . come out, those who have done good, will be raised to life and those who have done evil acts will be raised to stand trial" (5:28, 29).

The majority of Christians needed proof, including the absurd statement that Jesus had something to eat and drink after his resurrection. Most likely the religious experience, including that of one's own resurrection in the present, posed a serious threat to the whole dogmatic system. In addition, it would have made the whole church difficult to rule. The insistence on bodily resurrection, which depended on proper conduct within the church, had a political dimension.

With these comments I have made a sweeping step into the second and third generation of Christians. Now it is time to move back to the only Christian of the first generation who himself left documents behind, Paul, in order further to study the dynamics of the early Christian experience. It is only after having examined Paul that we shall return to the Gnostics again.

When Paul turned from a persecutor to a preacher of the gospel, he joined a movement shaped by the conviction that the return of Jesus on the clouds of heaven was imminent. That follows from the content of the earliest of Paul's letters, 1 Thessalonians. In this letter he takes it for granted that he will be among the survivors without having to experience death first. The other few Christians who had died would be raised at the coming of Jesus to make up for the disadvantage of premature death. After that the rapture would occur: both the minority of raised Christians and the majority of surviving Christians, including Paul, would be lifted up to meet the Lord Jesus in the air.

It does not take a lot of intelligence to say that sooner or later such an expectation faced serious difficulties. All of us know (for otherwise we would not be here or even live on this earth) that Jesus did not come back and that, consequently, the first Christian generation died away, including Paul.

How would Paul respond to the failure of the imminent expectation? Would he give up his belief in Jesus? If not, how would he be able to cope with the new situation of an ever increasing number of dead Christians in his communities?

All of you will remember Paul's words in one of his later letters: 'to live is Christ and to die is gain" (Phil 1:21). Paul continues a little later: "I desire to depart and to be with Christ, which is better by far. But it is more necessary for you that I remain in the body" (Phil 1:23, 24). Obviously, at the time of Philippians he had the hope of being united with Christ immediately after death whereas at the time of 1 Thessalonians this union would take place without delay at the return of Jesus on the clouds of heaven. That is quite a shift and cries out for an explanation. How and for what reason was Paul able to make such a change? Its reason is quite clear: If Paul had not succeeded in adjusting, he would have lost his faith. But, he wanted to continue to believe. (Who gives up heavenly reward easily?) The solution of the questions may be found in the nature of Paul's experience. He had seen what he calls Christ in a vision near Damascus, and this Christ-experience became stronger in his life almost on a daily basis. In this experience the non-destructibility of the new life was implied. It is therefore no wonder that this new life which was given by Christ to Paul at his conversion, being Christ himself, would have to be united again with Christ at the moment of Paul's death. Observing what was going on in Paul's psyche after Damascus, one can see, I think, a dramatic drive towards a complete fulfillment of life at the end of which there stands a new humanity (consisting of all human beings united with the cosmic Christ).

Let me now pick up the thread that I left when I turned from the Gnostics of the second and third generation to the only Christian of the first generation who has left written sources behind. Most of these gnostics admired Paul very much. They were the ones who developed Paul's line of thought. In a newly discovered gnostic writing, the letter to Rheginus (from NHC I,4), the unknown author describes resurrection as transferal to the original status of humanity, that is, as coming to him/herself. In the process of being raised, Christians receive themselves as they were from the beginning. "Resurrection" is not to be understood literally, of course. Rather it is an image of something which remains stable and is being activated through the knowledge of what the Christians were at the very beginning. Therefore the author of the letter to Rheginus asks the addressee: "Why not consider yourself as risen (into the realm of imperishability from where you come and to which you belong)?"

A parallel to this kind of interpretation of the resurrection can be found in the way in which the Gnostics understand the kingdom of God. A tractate from Nag Hammadi is again very illuminating in that respect. In the Gospel of Thomas, (saying 113), we read: "Jesus' disciples said to him: When will the kingdom come? (Jesus said:) It will not come by waiting for it. It will not be a matter of saying 'here it is' or 'there it is'. Rather the kingdom of the father is spread out on the earth, and men do not see it." Compare another saying from the same gospel on the same subject, saying 3:

If those who lead you, say to you, "See the kingdom is in the sky", then the birds of the sky will precede you. If they say to you, "It is in the sea", then the fish will precede you. Rather the kingdom is inside of you, and it is outside of you. When you come to know yourselves, then you will become known and you will realize that it is you who are the sons of the living father. But if you will not know yourselves, you dwell in poverty and it is you who are that poverty.

In other words, both the resurrection and the kingdom of god are something in the present that should be grasped and discovered. It is worth searching for saying as 2 shows: "Jesus said: 'Let him who seeks continue seeking until he finds. When he finds, he will become troubled. When he becomes troubled, he will be astonished, and he will rule over the All."

The same power, strength and, indeed, omnipotence which is being given to the believer receives attention in two other words of Jesus from the Gospel of Thomas.

Jesus said: If two make peace with each other in this one house, they will say to the mountain: Move away, and it will move away. (Logion 48)

Jesus said: When you make the two one, you will become the sons of Adam, and when you say: Mountain, move away, it will move away. (Logion 106)

The message of these two sayings of Jesus in the framework of the gospel of Thomas is as follows: Whenever the gnostic goal of restoring unity is achieved, the phenomenon of a faith that moves mountains comes into the picture.

It is a well-founded hypothesis that the saying about a faith that moves mountains goes back to the historical Jesus. It is preserved in both Mark 11:23 and Q (Matt 17:20b/Luke 17:6) and it is not attested in the Jewish tradition apart from 1 Cor 13:2. It reads in the Markan version:

Amen, I say to you, Whoever says to this mountain, 'Lift yourself up and cast yourself into the sea!' and does not doubt in his heart, but believes that what he says will come true, to him it will be granted!"

This saying is of such elemental force, it penetrates so deeply to the basic relations of being, that it reflects an original mind. In addition I am also tempted to regard the saying in Mark (11:24) as authentic. It reads: "Therefore I say to you: Whatever you pray and ask for, believe that you have received (it), and it will be granted to you."

Let me hasten to add that most likely the phrase "your faith/trust has saved you" which is part of healing stories (Mark 5:34; 10:52) also goes back to the historical Jesus, although its connection with the stories is secondary. At the same time it must be emphasized that in the gospel tradition the historical Jesus is never an object of faith, the only example being the expression "faith in Jesus" in Matt 18:6, clearly an interpretation of Mark 9:42, where we hear about the little ones who have faith/trust.

We seem to have three groups of authentic sayings of Jesus which are related to faith: a) the faith that moves mountains, b) the faith that is related to prayer, c) the faith that leads to healing.

What is the nature of such an understanding of faith?

From the very beginning it has to be emphasized that the root of the power of these three understandings of faith is God. However, it must be acknowledged that Jesus does not mention God when he talks about faith. As a Jew of his time, Jesus' understanding of faith must have been related to his understanding of God, all the more so because Jesus surely prayed to God and to nobody else. When he prayed he looked to heaven where, according to the worldview of his time, God was residing with his angels. In addition, Jesus must have known the Shema Israel, which, as a minimum requirement according to Josephus (Ant. IV 212), every Jew had to speak twice a day, early in the morning and before going to sleep. Here is the text: "Hear O Israel, the Lord our God is one Lord" (Deut 5:4). To this is added the divine commandment: "And you shall love the Lord your God with all your heart, and with all your soul, and with all your might. And these words which I command you this day shall be on your heart; and you shall teach them diligently to your children, and shall talk of them when you sit in your house, and when you walk by the way, and when you lie down, and when you rise," (Deut 6:5–7).

A third element in Jesus' prayer life is even more important. I am thinking of Jesus' understanding of God whom he addressed as his heavenly father. This father was a loving one and Jesus' deep conviction was that the eternal, distant, dominating Creator is also and primarily a near and approachable god. Jesus' familial expression for god as Abba, without any further qualifications suggestive of transcendence (Lord or King in heaven who has created the universe) certainly points to a religious experience of deep intimacy with God. (Such a statement does not necessarily imply, by the way, that Jesus called God Daddy.)

Given this context of Jesus' understanding of God, it is noteworthy that his own understanding of faith is similarly deeply rooted in the Jewish tradition. Faith cannot be understood without its background in the Old Testament. Here we find the linguistic root: Hebrew, *aemet* for Jesus' understanding of faith. *Aemet* means trust and the related word *amen* means "it holds" or "it is true". The larger context, in the theology of the Hebrew Bible, is that trust, law, justice, creation and the election of Israel are closely associated. God, according to such thinking, is holding his creation together through justice, trust and his law. The Israelites answer God's call by trusting God in order to live. We have a key passage in the book of Isaiah where in a time of political crisis the prophet tells the king Ahaz: "If you do not believe, you will not remain" (Isa 7:9b). Other translations are as follows: "If you do not trust, you will not remain entrusted" (M. Buber); "If you do not believe, you will not abide" (RSV). The interesting thing is that both verbs, believe/trust and stand/remain, have the same linguistic root, *aemet*, and express different aspects of time (*Hiphil* and *Niphal*). The prophet Isaiah is playing with words here, most likely on purpose. At the historical level he tells Ahaz not to look for any political coalition but to hold on to a quiet trust which takes into account the reality of God's faithfulness. At a deeper level I would dare to say that from this understandings of faith we learn that Jewish and Christian understanding of faith both are rooted in the tradition of the Hebrew Bible and are closely related to what philosophers call Being. Faith has to do with what establishes existence, gives it subsistence. The question therefore is "to be or not to be," since faith is that in which our existence receives its ground. That, however, is possible only because God ensures such an order and makes the believer participate in his omnipotence. Note the order: first God, then human being.

After Jesus had died a bloody death on the cross, the disciples did not continue Jesus' life rooted in faith. After only a brief period of grief, they overcame his sudden death by claiming that God had raised him from the dead, something which Christians from then on had to believe. That belief constituted their faith. Despite the difference from Jesus on this point, it remains noteworthy that in both cases God played a key role. The disciples' and especially Paul's proclamation led to a new dimension of faith that was centered on a specific doctrine, Jesus' resurrection, however absurd that sounded in the ears of the educated of the first century. At the same time, both Jesus and his disciples affirmed that God had elected Israel though such a statement was shifted by the early church to the doctrine that God had elected the church and had therefore rejected unbelieving Israel. Despite the change concerning the election, God remained the same and the structure of thought remained identical in that the election of a specific group of people was claimed, in contrast with the *massa damnationis*.

Such matters had to come under attack as soon as Christianity reached the educated classes of the Roman empire. The second century Platonic philosopher Celsus wrote an attack against Christianity in which he tells his readers about Christian missionaries: they take advantage of the lack of education of gullible people and lead them wherever they wish, demanding nothing else but faith. "Do not ask questions; just believe. Your faith will save you. The wisdom in the world is an evil, and foolishness is a good thing" (cCels I:9). Also the specific doctrine of election comes under attack. Celsus writes the following parody about Jews and Christians:

> The race of the Jews and of the Christians is like a cluster of bats or ants coming out of a nest, or frogs holding council round a marsh, or worms assembling in some filthy corner, disagreeing with one another about which of them are the worse sinners. They say: God shows and proclaims everything to us beforehand, and he has even deserted the whole world and the motion of heavens, and disregarded the vast earth to give attention to us alone; and he sends messengers to us alone and never stops sending them and seeking that we may be with him for ever. There is God first, and we are next after him in rank since he has made us entirely like God, and all things have been put under us, earth, water, air, and stars; and all things exist for our benefit, and have been appointed to serve us. (cCels IV:23).

As this second-century philosopher rightly wrote, it is just a matter of education that specific Christian doctrines, including those of Jesus fall apart. First of all, as Celsus correctly remarked, the idea of being elected by God stinks and has created nothing but counter claims and hostility leading to acts of aggression.

In a fictional letter to Jesus I pointed out to him another aspect of the matter: "Perhaps you would have become pensive had you learned that heaven is not above you, that the earth is a globe and not the center of the Universe. And probably you would have been very surprised to learn that human beings and apes have common ancestors, indeed that all existing species of living beings are part of a development which began with primitive unicellular organisms. And you would certainly have panicked had you been aware that even 2000 years after you, your God had still not brought in an end of the ages. And not only that: your God did not even create the world, as you had to assume as a pious Jew of your day. Rather, the universe came into being through an evolution which according to our present-day knowledge began with a Big Bang. The image of a creator God which you and your contemporaries had was shaped far too much from a human perspective . . ." Let me hasten to add a remark from the pre-Socratic philosopher Xenophanes who once said: "If the oxes could paint, their god would have the image of an ox."

At the same time, Jesus' idea of faith and the idea of faith in the Hebrew Bible have something appealing even for modern people: Faith understood as trust, being rooted in the ground of being, standing firm, sheds light on a basic human need. Small children have a basic need for trust or primary love, as research has shown. In other words, what the Hebrew Bible, going back to older semitic ideas — and Jesus presupposed and elaborate rings true to every human being who lives in today's world. At the same time all of us have little sympathy for the theocentric context in which these ideas once stood. We live in a secular world and in which god has been banished from everyday life. Most of us do pretty well without him. Anyone of us who during a psychoanalytical session used the name God too often would trigger the suspicion of a religiously motivated neurosis. In addition, any biblical doctrine about the good creation of this world, as the bible tells us, makes us pause. What should we make of a creation in which the routine activity is for organisms to tear others apart with teeth and claws. Creation is a nightmare spectacular taking place on a planet that has been soaked for hundreds of million of years in the blood of all its creatures. And we have been thrown into this life, indeed sentenced to life, without previously being asked.

Being torn between the absurdities of this life and an attraction to a human reading of Jesus' message of faith, let me continue our journey through the faith traditions of early Christianity and move one last time to the Gnostic view of these things. Among the Nag Hammadi texts we encounter a group whose members called themselves "the unwavering race." Defining themselves in such a way, they claimed to have discovered a status of permanent stability. The claim to belong to the unwavering race goes hand in hand with a distancing from the creator of this world, the biblical God. No other text of the Hebrew Bible is so often and negatively quoted as the self-declaration of the biblical God in Isaiah (45:5): "I am a jealous God, and there is no other beside me." Such a claim was, according to the members of the unwavering race, arrogant, sinful and the product of a blind mind. In these gnostic texts, to be members of the immovable race means that one's stability is not assured by trust in the creator, but rather is threatened by it. (According to the Gospel of Philip, the creator and his archons even tried to divert the thought of the Gnostics from the stable to the unstable by a confusion of names.) Instead the achievement of immovability (and the restitution of stability) is viewed as the result of human potential, the truly human being the mind and spirit of the unbegotten Son of Man, and not the flesh and bones or the animal passions. The immovable race, as portrayed in myth, pre-exists the appearance of the physical world of historical experience. And this being interpreted means: the human potentialities that are pre-supposed in all particular worldly experiences. The members of the immovable race have come to know themselves and their true origin. They are sparks of the God "Man." In principle their movement is open to everybody, transcending the human borders of religion, culture and politics.

Conclusion

We have reached the end of our journey through the bizarre world of a variety of religious experiences. I started with a personal glance backwards at my conversion experience and continued by looking at how liberal theologians then and now deal with the dynamics of faith. While they were intellectually right on the rebuttal of the Bible by historical criticism, their own theology seems to me to be anemic to the highest degree. In order to recover the early Christian experience we looked at the Gnostics and their reinterpretation of the resurrection, then to the apostle Paul whose letters are a litmus test for any approach to early Christianity as the only Christian of the first generation who has left sources behind. It was only after such a detour that we took a detailed look at Jesus' experience of faith and its presuppositions, the notion of a loving God and the Hebrew understanding of faith. We recovered a complete ontology with some features (faith as trust, stability, rootedness) that appeal to the modern person. And finally the gnostic idea of self-knowledge on the basis of belonging to the immovable race avoids the shortcomings of Jesus' belief in a creator father god and preserves the human appeal that it still has if it is read from a human level: to provide and open up an area of stability, depth and steadfastness.

Let me now try to offer a constructive synthesis of my own: Man does not live by the bread of historical facts and technology alone. We have to go deeper and search for the foundation of our life. We look for the ground of being for, by and on which we can stand in order to affirm ourselves in the face of the terror of life and creation. Faith, understood as a rootedness in Being, incorporates its power and is effective in every act of courage on the face of this earth. Faith becomes knowledge once heaven is opened up again and liberated from a creator god who wants to keep humans from looking beyond him. After having gone deep down and thereby having rediscovered the ground on which we can stand and whereby stability is provided, we can finally move up into the immense space of the Universe which has been opened up again. Then our life acquires a truly cosmic dimension and we finally experience the taste for the Infinite. We become part of the race of the free spirits. For us the way up and the way down are the same. In the realm of true Being all distinctions cease to exist. The approach to this is the way of negation in which we come to realize that all categories and classifications are illusions, false perceptions. We achieve our end when each of our own formulations loses value. In the complete nothingness of human categories we find the all and the only reality. The Light of Being can come to us only when the light of human thought is extinguished. So the ultimate could be called Darkness, the Cloud of Unknowing, interchangeably with Light or Gnosis.

These phrases are not meant to make me out an apophantic mystic who claims to possess secret knowledge. However, they echo the experience of specific situations where I felt myself in tune with the universe. Such peak experiences were possible only after a liberation from my own dogmatic tradition which, as well as any other religious tradition from now on, has to pass the test of modernity. "Even if the open windows of science at first make us shiver with cold after the cosy indoor warmth of traditional humanizing myths, in the end the fresh air brings vigour, and the great spaces have a splendour of their own" (Bertrand Russell).

Notes

* I have left the text of my lecture as it was presented. The historical evaluations of the texts that were cited and analysed are based on my new book: *Jesus after 2000 Years. What He Really Said and Did.* (London: SCM Press/Amherst, NY: Prometheus, 2000). For information on the conflict at my home University of Göttingen, one may consult my book: *The Great Deception. And What Jesus really Said and Did* (Prometheus Books), 1999, pp. ix–xxii. Since the time of the remarks in the book the conflict has heated up and is now before a court of law. See my webpage (www.gwdg.de/~gluedem/) for further details. My book *The Great Deception* also contains "A Letter to Jesus" (the quotation in the text is taken from pp. 5–6) which started all the trouble.

Walter Wink

the Son of Man
the Stone that Builders Rejected

Dedicated to Elizabeth Boyden Howes

T he Jesus Seminar has not been exactly kind to the son of the man. Of the 84 instances of this phrase in the gospels, the Seminar voted none red, 3 pink, 9 gray, and 72 black. And in the *Five Gospels* translation the Seminar rendered "the son of the man" as "son of Adam," thus missing what I would regard as the heart of the matter. I would like to persuade you that this stone that the builders rejected will become the head of the corner.

There has been another set of seminars in this neighborhood: the seminars on the Records of the Life of Jesus offered by the Guild for Psychological Studies in San Francisco. I have found the insights of the founder, Elizabeth Boyden Howes, and of her mentor, Carl Jung, fundamental to everything in this paper, and it is with deepest gratitude and respect that I dedicate this lecture to her.

There are few mysteries in biblical studies as unfathomable as the expression, "the son of the man." Scarcely any topic in all research has received more attention, and with less result. Here are the few facts that define the problem. "Son of man" (without definite articles) appears 108 times in the Hebrew Scriptures, 93 of them in Ezekiel. Curiously, God refuses to call Ezekiel by his given name, but addresses him only as "son of man." No one else calls Ezekiel "son of man," only God.

A similar expression appears in the New Testament some 87 times, all but three in the gospels (Mark 14, Matthew 31, Luke 26, John 13). Counting the parallels only once (25 paralleled, 15 unparalleled), the Synoptic instances are compressed to 40. When these are added to the 13 in John, we have a total of 53 different sayings in the gospels which feature this enigmatic expression.[1]

This barbaric Greek idiom, *ho huios tou anthropou*, is so awkward that virtually all translators omit the second definite article.[2] You may be wondering why I render the Greek expression in the gospels "the son of *the* man." Quite simply, I do so because that is what the Greek phrase says, and it should be translated that way, despite a conspiracy of translators to render it with only one definite article. To add insult to injury, they also add caps where there are none. I will render the expression literally, with both articles, to underscore its oddness and crudity. I apologize on behalf of the New Testament for the double sexism in this expression.

In the gospels, "the son of the man" always appears exclusively on the lips of Jesus.[3] No one else addresses him by this expression. It is not a title used about him by others. It is not employed as a christological designation or confession by his disciples.

Herein lies the puzzle. Jesus apparently avoided designation as messiah, son of God, or God, though these titles were given to him after his death and resurrection by his disciples. But Jesus is repeatedly depicted as using the obscure expression "the son of the man" as virtually his only form of self-reference. Yet his disciples after his death almost completely ignored the expression. Paul never once used it, nor any of the writers of other epistles. It appears only a few times in the Apostolic Fathers. So far as we know, no one worshiped "the son of the man" or made that figure the one addressed in prayer. In so far as the expression was used by the later church, it was merely amalgamated with the other christological titles, or treated as an expression indicating Jesus' human, as opposed to his divine, nature. "The son of the man" was never made the basis of any church confession, never appears in any of the church's creeds, and in time virtually disappeared from usage.

Furthermore, the expression appears very seldom in other Jewish sources of the period. It is used a few times in the Dead Sea Scrolls, sixteen times in the Similitudes section of the First Book of Enoch, and once in 4 Ezra. In rabbinic sources some 500 years later the expression appears a few times. The Gnostics alone used the expression frequently. But only in the gospels is it exclusively a way in which Jesus speaks of himself. No attempt to unravel this mystery that ignores the uniqueness and intensity of this usage concentrated on Jesus, and seeks instead a solution in general linguistics, can hope to succeed.

Nevertheless, the tendency of scholarly discussion in the last decades has been to attempt precisely such a linguistic solution. The conclusion of the philologists who have been laboring over this question recently is that the expression has no theological meaning whatever, but is just a circumlocution for "I" or "me" or "one" or "myself and people like me." Such a conclusion simply sidesteps the fact that no one but Jesus made this phrase the exclusive manner of his self-designation.[4] Only in Ezekiel and the gospels is the phrase associated with a particular person; yet Ezekiel never refers to himself as "son of man" as Jesus does. Obviously it was inevitable that indirect forms of self address would occasionally crop up in Palestinian Aramaic sources; such forms of address appear in many languages. One need look no farther than the 1996 U.S. presidential election, in which Republican candidate Bob Dole repeatedly spoke of himself in the third person ("Bob Dole won't raise your taxes"). Such elliptical forms of self-address have a variety of functions (not wishing to appear to boast, or as a self-deprecating way of speaking about oneself, or just as a manner of speaking of oneself in general terms — "Can't a person have any privacy?").[5] But it is inconceivable that Jesus experienced such occasions with such frequency when no one else did. Morna Hooker ponders, "If the phrase was a common expression for 'I' in Aramaic, then the use of the barbaric Greek phrase [ho huios tou anthro{long o}pou] seems an inexplicable blunder; the fact that it was thought necessary to use this translationese suggests that there was already something a little unusual and special about the Aramaic equivalent [bar enasha], even in an Aramaic-speaking community."[6] The rabbinic parallels, far from providing a general explanation that illuminates Jesus' usage, leave us even more deeply in the dark as to why Jesus, in a way uncharacteristic of any other person, makes himself — or is made — the focus of this odd manner of self-designation.

In fact, all "the son of the man" sayings in the gospels could be rendered by "I" if the so-called apocalyptic passages are regarded as Jesus speaking of himself and not another. The easy way out, chosen by some recent scholars, is simply to opt for mistranslation, and regard "the son of the man" as nothing more than an indirect form of self-reference.[7] But why then did the evangelists not use "I" consistently, since they unmistakably thought "the son of the man" meant "I" in at least some cases? Jesus shows no hesitation whatever in using "I"; he does so scores of times. "I" could have appeared in all the son of the man sayings and we never would have missed "the son of the man" or guessed that it once stood there. We can scarcely argue that "the son of the man" is a mistranslation;

anyone even remotely capable of rendering a sentence from Aramaic into Greek would know perfectly well that "son of" is an idiomatic expression meaning simply "of or pertaining to the following genus or species." So if "son of man" means simply "human being" or "person" or "mortal," why were the definite articles added? Why was the expression preserved at all?

The most extreme position is that taken by those scholars — among them the majority of the Jesus Seminar — who simply dismiss all son of the man sayings as creations of the early church, and thus as without interest for the quest of the historical Jesus. I find it simply inconceivable that a church which made absolutely no use of the "son of the man" in other contexts would have invented some 84 references to it, spread about evenly among all four gospels — 84 times in only 121 pages (NRSV), translated in exactly the same form (with but one exception — John 5:27). And it is always *only* Jesus that uses it. At the time the gospels were written, the more exalted christological titles (Messiah/Christ, Son of God, God) were already fully deployed and served as the basis both for christological reflection and liturgical celebration. So why would the church create so many son of the man sayings at a time when no one was using that expression of Jesus in the life of the churches? Certainly there must have been a critical mass of authentic sayings of such potency as to trigger creative additions to the fund of already existing sayings. If the church had invented the son of the man sayings, it would not have used two articles. Rather, it would have used *no* articles in order to create a proof from prophecy that pointed directly to Ezekiel and Dan 7:13.

Perhaps it would help to say what the "son of the man" is not. In the time prior to Jesus, it was not the title of an apocalyptic figure expected to come to earth to judge and redeem humanity. Nor was the pre-Christian "son of the man" a messianic deliverer.[8] It had not been amalgamated with the Suffering Servant of Isaiah 53. It was not a heaven-appointed judge who would preside over the last judgment. In Daniel it was a divine figure to whom God gives dominion and authority, but it was not yet developed as it would later be in the New Testament, where it is made a prophecy of the Second Coming of Christ.

This much at least is clear: Jesus did not use "the son of the man" as a self-deprecating expression of humility. If there is anything Jesus was not, it was modest. Few people ever spoke with such unmediated authority, or made a higher claim than Jesus: that he was ushering the Reign of God into the world. We will come to Jesus in due time. But first we need to set Jesus' use of this strange third-person self-reference in its context in the Hebrew Bible.

The Son of Man in the Hebrew Bible

Idiomatically, the Hebrew term *ben adam*, "son of man," simply means "human being." But the pressure of theological reflection surrounding Jesus' use of the expression has, until recently, led translators to leave the phrase in its confusing idiomatic form. Newer translations of the Hebrew Scriptures now consistently render the expression in good English: "mere man" or "mortal man" (TEV), "a human being" or "O man" (REB), "mortal(s)," "the one" (NRSV), or "son of Adam." My own suggestion is that we render "son of man" by the term "HumanBeing."

Briefly, Psalm 8 speaks of humanity as "son of man" (*ben adam*) in both its insignificance and its cosmic grandeur. Psalm 80 underscores the term's ambiguity, since it can represent Israel, or a king, or a messianic deliverer, or (as the church later concluded), Jesus. This oscillation between personal and collective denotations is characteristic of this expression in many of the texts that use it, suggesting that there is something intrinsic about its ambiguity.

Most important, however, is Ezekiel. No other book of the Bible even approaches Ezekiel in the number of its references to the son of man — 93. In Ezekiel's vision of the divine throne chariot, we encounter the most significant vision in the Bible, indeed, one of the most influential visions in all of human history.

This vision is the fountainhead of Jewish mysticism. An entire library of writings derives from it right up to the present — an unbroken chain of esoteric traditions lasting 2,500 years.

I want to focus on just one aspect of this rich vision (Ezek 1:26–2:1):

> And above the dome over their heads there was something like a throne, in appearance like sapphire; and seated above the likeness of a throne was something that seemed like a human form. Upward from what appeared like the loins I saw something like gleaming amber, something that looked like fire enclosed all around; and downward from what looked like the loins I saw something that looked like fire, and there was a splendor all around. Like the bow in a cloud

on a rainy day, such was the appearance of the splendor all around. This was the appearance of the likeness of the glory of the Lord.

"When I saw it, I fell on my face, and I heard the voice of someone speaking. He said to me: O mortal (*ben adam*), stand up on your feet, and I will speak with you.

At the center of this vision, the qualifications and hesitations stumble all over themselves: "And above the dome over their heads there was *something like* a throne, *in appearance like* sapphire; and seated above the *likeness* of a throne was *something* that *seemed like* a human form."

And this is the revelation: God seems to be, as it were, Human.

This is not just a figure of speech. Israel was thoroughly familiar with figures of speech, and never confused them with reality. If you asked Jews if God was walking in the Garden of Eden in the cool of the day because the noonday heat was disagreeable (Gen. 3:8), they would have dismissed the question as impertinent: Of course not, that is only a figure of speech.

But Ezekiel is not beholding a figure of speech. God really seems to be turning a human face toward Ezekiel. Whatever else God might be in the wildness of nature and the blackness of interstellar space, when God wishes to manifest divine reality to Ezekiel, it is in "the likeness as it were of a human form."

What does it mean to say that God is revealed as human? Why, does God turn a human-like face to Ezekiel? Perhaps because becoming human is the task that God has set for human beings. And human beings have only a vague idea what it means to be human. Humanity errs in believing that it is human. We are only fragmentarily human, fleetingly human, brokenly human. We see glimpses of our humanness, we can dream of what a more humane existence and political order would be like, but we have not yet arrived at true humanness. Ezekiel's vision intimates that only God is, as it were, Human, and since we are made in God's image and likeness, we are capable of becoming more truly human ourselves. As Gerd Theissen notes, people were once especially eager to find the "missing link" between primates and human beings. Now, however, it is dawning on us that we ourselves could be that "missing link."[9]

Furthermore, we are incapable of becoming human by ourselves. We scarcely know what humanness is. We have only the merest intuitions and general guidelines. Jesus has, to be sure, revealed to us what it means to live a fully human life. But how do I translate that into my own struggles for humanness? Curiously, I know more about God, thanks to Jesus, than I do about myself. Metaphysically speaking, God is the ultimate mystery, but to myself I am an even more impenetrable mystery. Who am I? I have accepted my parents' answers, my culture's answers, the answers of mentors and peers and colleagues. But how do they know? What are the exact outlines of my true form? What is the visage of my real face? How can I find out, unless God reveals it to me? For who else could possibly know what is stored up in the divine image inside me, except that One who is the divine image inside me? As one of the most remarkable lines of Scripture puts it, "Beloved, we are God's children now; what we will be has not yet been revealed. What we do know is this: when HumanBeing is revealed, we will be like it, for we will see it as it is" (1 John 3:2*).[10]

Perhaps someday we might become more fully human. For now, we are only promissory notes, hints, intimations. But we are able to become more human because the Human One has placed within us the divine spirit (Ezek 37:5, 14).

If God is in some sense true humanness, then divinity inverts. Divinity is not a qualitatively different reality; quite the reverse, *divinity is fully realized humanity*. Only God is, as it were, HUMAN. The goal of life, then, is not to become something we are not — divine — but to become what we truly are — human. We are not required to become divine: flawless, perfect, without blemish. We are invited simply to become human, which means growing through our mistakes, learning by trial and error, being redeemed over and over from sin and compulsive behavior, becoming ourselves, scars and all. It means embracing and transforming our shadow side. It means giving up pretending to be good and instead becoming real. In this vision, then, God represents the archetypal image, "as it were," of individuated human being, reaching out through Ezekiel to God's people with a humanly impossible task: that of becoming human.

Eastern Orthodoxy has long taught that the goal of human existence is to become "divinized." I have deep respect for the spiritual disciplines that the orthodox mystics have developed in order to further this process of growth into God. But I have no idea what divinization signifies. When people say Jesus is divine, or the Son of God, or God, I have nothing in my experience that can help me comprehend what they mean. It all sounds too much like the language of Greek polytheism, in which gods impregnated mortal women, who bore beings who were half human and half divine. The interminable debates about the two natures of Christ seem to me to be totally off the mark, an irrelevancy carried over from a worldview that is now virtually defunct for all but the truest of true believers, and a stumbling block to all dialogue with other religions. I do not know what the word divine signifies. But I do have an inkling of what the word "human" might entail, because we are made in the image of God, the Human One, and there have been exemplary human beings, in our tradition and that of others.

Central to the Eastern Orthodox tradition is a statement by the church father Athanasius that Christ became as we are that we might become as he is. This has usually been interpreted as meaning that Christ became human that we might become divine. I hear it saying rather that Jesus became like us — people living within the constraints of earthly reality — in order that we might become like him — fully human. But that way of speaking is still too mythologically literal for me. I would prefer to say, Jesus incarnated God in his own person in order to show all of us how to incarnate God. And to incarnate God is what it means to be fully human.

But we risk loosing the numinous reality under a barrage of words. Ezekiel was not struck by an interesting new idea. He was, rather, struck to the ground. The vision overwhelms him, like a blow to the solar plexus.

When the One-as-it-were-in-human-form now addresses Ezekiel, it does so as a parent to a child: "*Ben adam* ["child of the Human One"], stand up on your feet and I will speak with you." As a "chip off the old Block," this offspring of the HUMAN will from henceforth not be addressed by his given name, but only as the child of the Enthroned One. In the moment that one faces the Glory of God, the Offspring of the Human is born. To see God as Human is to begin to become what one sees, for as the Guild's Richard Naegle taught me, our image of God creates us. What is born is a person able to face and to carry this numinous power. The HumanBeing is thus related somehow to the divine image or *imago dei* as an aspect of the Self archetype. It bears that within us that has been potential from the beginning but that has not yet come to conscious awareness and accessibility. By addressing the prophet as "offspring of the Human One," God indicates that humanizing humanity is one of God's central concerns.

What Ezekiel saw was the human face of God, God as humanity needs to know God in order to become what God calls us to be. We become what our desire beholds. So the mystic is one who chooses to seek the God who freely offers us the gift of our own humanity, not as something to be attained, but as pure revelation. God is, as it were, a mirror in which we find reflected our own "heavenly," that is, our potential, face.

Jesus and the Humanbeing

Much more needs to be said, but we must now turn to the New Testament to see how "the son of the man" is used there. A number of scholars early in the twentieth century were convinced that the biblical "son of man" was an offshoot of Iranian mythology about an "Urmensch" or Original Man.[11] Subsequent research has exposed the synthetic nature of this "myth," which never existed in the form proposed. Despite the complete absence of such a hypothetical myth anywhere in pre-Christian sources, there is something irreducibly mythic about this mysterious figure. It glows with a halo of overdetermined meaning. What we seem to have is a mythic figure without a myth. It was the seminal contribution of Elizabeth Boyden Howes, following the lead of her mentor Jung, to recognize that the "son of the man" was not a title or a nickname or a circumlocution or a myth, but an *archetypal image*. As an archetypal image it functions as a symbol of wholeness, less august and almighty than the Messiah or Christ, more mundane and daily than the heroes of myth, more a catalytic agent of transformation in the service of the Self than a symbol of the Self as such.[12]

Howes continues,

> . . . the term 'Son of man' is related to but is not the same as the archetype of the Self . . . It was used by Jesus to describe the main image which dominated his life and which can be found by others, as it describes in a rather rare way the Self as it operated through him. The 'Son of man' phrase describes the Self *at work in concrete life*, a Self lived existentially, not as a hope or a vision; but it is not the same as the Self. We have thus a picture of God coming into humanity lived as the Son of man by Jesus.[13]

It is impossible in the limits of this lecture to provide the exegetical grounding that alone would make that hypothesis persuasive. Briefly, I regard the so-called earthly son of the man sayings as on the whole reliable, though that has to be settled case by case. But it seems altogether implausible that a church that already was regarding Jesus as ascended to the right hand of the Power of God would then create sayings and stories that emphasize Jesus' lowliness. Likewise, while no extant prediction of the passion may be preserved verbatim, I do believe that Jesus said something like "the son of the man must suffer many things and be rejected." One redactional statement by Matthew gives us a rare insight into what at least one evangelist thought about the "son of the man." In the story of the healing of the paralytic Matt 9:2–8, Jesus has just said that "the son of the man has authority on earth to forgive sins." In reporting the acclamation of the crowd, Matthew makes this astonishing statement: "and they glorified God, who had given such authority to" — and here we would expect Matthew of all people to finish the clause with "Christ" or at least "Jesus." Instead he has "human beings" (the Hebrew equivalent would be *bene adam*). The HumanBeing is not, then, restricted to Jesus, but includes his disciples and, indeed, anyone who is in relationship with the process of becoming whole. So also, in the plucking of grain on the sabbath (Mark 2:23–28), it is not Jesus, but the disciples, who take upon themselves the right to decide when the sabbath is being broken.

Such sovereign freedom, placed in the hands of the underclasses, inevitably strikes terror in the hearts of those entrusted with the tranquility of society. The dramatic location of the initiation of the death plot against Jesus only a few verses after the story of the plucking of the grain in Mark (3:6) may or may not be chronologically exact, but it is logically appropriate. It was not simply the religious and political authorities who trembled at the human cost of such freedom, however. The early church also blanched at so much moral discretion being placed at the disposal of common people. Hence Matthew and Luke omit Mark 2:27 ("the sabbath was made for humankind . . . "). But v. 27 is the original connection to verse 23–24, since it alone responds to the initial controversy. By deleting that verse, Matthew and Luke have converted the saying into its opposite: the assertion that Jesus *alone* as "the Son of Man" is lord of the sabbath. Once "the son of the man" had been flattened into a mere equivalent of Son of God and Christ/Messiah, no other reading seemed possible. Whereas special *need* had originally justified the breach or suspension of the law, now one's relationship with a special *person* does so — a person endowed with a transcendent authority shared by no one else.

God transcendent is God immanent in the HumanBeing. Jesus does not contemplate a God outside the universe intervening to heal the paralytic, but as a power which can be evoked in the sick person himself. That power is put into action by their acts: take up your bed and walk! What Jesus says arouses the HumanBeing in the other. Jesus knows that the HumanBeing has its locus in himself, but it also has its locus in the paralytic. The HumanBeing seems to function as a kind of immanent principle of eschatological wholeness, or, more simply, as the mediator and actualizer of God's intent for our becoming whole.

What then does Jesus give as the reason for listening to him? It would appear that his only claim on his hearers was the fact that he acted and spoke with authority (*exousia* — "out of being," Mark 1:27). Was this not the source of the enormous sense of power in the early church, for which nothing in their previous experience had prepared them: that they themselves were "lords of the sabbath"? If through Jesus they had been put in touch with the HumanBeing within them, no wonder they had such collective self-confidence and indomitable courage. These lowly disciples of Jesus are authorized with a power that equals or exceeds that of the priesthood. And this power is not derivative. It is not conferred by heredity or ordination. It is directly from God. It is not even mediated by Jesus, though it is clearly evoked by him.

To exercise the authority to forgive sins is to assume the power that one already has, but which one was unaware of. And not just unaware of, but deprived of, systematically stripped of, by the power-needs of those religious authorities who hold a monopoly on the dispensation of God's grace. To claim the power to forgive sins is thus not only to restore the lost humanity of others, but to recover lost aspects of one's own humanity as well.

But when all authority is vested only in Jesus, what becomes of the sovereign freedom that Jesus evoked in his disciples? What becomes of deciding for ourselves what is right (Luke 12:57)? It is indeed awesome how christology has been used to avoid the clear intent of Jesus! So the astonishing freedom of the HumanBeing was sabotaged in the interests of institutional harmony and rule by law.

Now, even if you were to find my historical argument unconvincing, and you still believe that the church created all the son of the man sayings, they would then simply represent one of the church's earliest christologies, and could still serve as the basis for a new son of the man christology from below.

We must slide over the rest of the son of the man sayings that deal with Jesus' authority, lowliness and death, and look briefly at the so-called apocalyptic sayings. These sayings should properly be separated into two piles, the *archetypal* and the *apocalyptic*. On the one hand, they depict Jesus as having ascended to the right hand of the Power of God. If we read this literally, as if Jesus rode a sunbeam back to God's throne room in the sky, it is virtually unintelligible. If, however, we take it as the accurate report of an archetypal mutation, it makes perfect sense. Something new had come to birth in the collective and personal psyches of the disciples. The HumanBeing whose divine power and authority they had seen incarnate in Jesus and occasionally in themselves, had now entered the heart of reality as a catalyst in the process of human transformation. The ascension is not grist for a discussion of miracles, because it was not a miracle. It marks an actual change in some people's perception of the divine. To see the HumanBeing ascended is thus to set our sights on what it means to become a human being. The HumanBeing "at the right hand of the Power" is the future of the species. "Seeing" this is to recognize that the HumanBeing as lived out by Jesus has entered the collective consciousness of humanity. Now it has become an archetypal image, capable of galvanizing unlived life and mobilizing untapped resistance to the institutions and structures that squeeze the life out of people. Picturing heaven as "up" is, of course, merely a convention of thought. But it well captures the sense that this figure, exalted from ignominious execution, shame, and abandonment, has become the "highest" value in the universe, the criterion of value itself, and the revelation of humanity's evolutionary goal, as Teilhard de Chardin saw so clairvoyantly. The slogan for this hope is that stunning passage in 1 John 3:2* already mentioned — "Beloved, we are God's children now; what we will be has not yet been revealed. What we do know is this: when HumanBeing is revealed, we will be like it, for we will see it as it is." The movement here is all toward God, following the pattern of Dan 7:13.

For his disciples, Jesus' death and ascension were like a black hole in space that sucked into its collapsing vortex the very meaning of the universe, until in the intensity of its compaction there was an explosive reversal, and the stuff of which galaxies are made was blown out into the universe. So Jesus' ascension to the right hand of the Power of God was a supernova in the archetypal sky. As the image of the truly Human One, Jesus became an exemplar of our own utmost possibilities for living.

The image of God, and other related images, thus underwent fundamental mutation. Jesus, as it were, infiltrated the Godhead. The very image of God was altered by the sheer force of Jesus' being. God was, in Jesus, taking on a human face. God would never be the same. Jesus indelibly imprinted the divine; God everlastingly entered the human. Following Jung, we might say that in Jesus, God took on humanity, furthering the evolution revealed in Ezekiel's vision of Yahweh on the throne in "the likeness, as it were, of a human form" (Ezek 1:26). From now on, Jesus' followers would experience God through the filter of Jesus. Jesus, people realized during his lifetime, is like God. God, they realized after his death, is now like Jesus. It is merely a prejudice of modern thought that events happen only in the outer world. What Christians regard as the most significant event in human history happened, according to the gospels, in the psychic realm, and it altered outer history irrevocably.

On the other hand, the *archetypal* HumanBeing was literalized into the *apocalyptic* notion of the second coming of the son of the man. The HumanBeing is no longer seen as both present and future. Rather, it is drenched with the symbolism of a longed-for wholeness in an indefinite future. The HumanBeing has become numinous, coming like a flash of lightning that illumines the sky from one end of heaven to another (Matt 24:27//Luke 17:24). Its power and glory are fearsome, and its judgments categorical. All these "son of the man" aspects, says Jung, are mythic, collective, unconscious, and as such, unrelated to individual consciousness. Forgiveness will not be a part of this final, future judgment. There will be no loving of enemies. The son of the man has lost all contact with the earth. Everything now takes place in the sky. The deep archetypal movement of images from the depth are pulled out and projected on a transcendent spiritual world as if on a cosmic screen. The urgency of deciding for or against the new order of Jesus has now become a call for unlimited and unending watchfulness, "for the son of the man is coming at an hour you do not expect" (Matt 24:44//Luke 12:40). The son of the man is identified with the figure of the Judge of all the world, whose judgments separated sheep from goats for an otherworldly heaven and hell (Matt 25:31–46). On his return, Jesus would do all the things he resolutely refused to do the first time around. Jesus would come again as world ruler, using all necessary force to coerce humanity into obedience to the divine purposes. It appears that God's immortal patience will have finally run out, and that all the weapons in the arsenal of righteousness will be used to devastating effect by the Supreme Commander of the heavenly hosts. This heavenly "son of the man" is a long, long way from the Galilean teacher who renounced violence in the name of a nonviolent God.

Thus depersonalized and deprived of real immediacy, the HumanBeing dropped from devotional life and from the life of the church generally. Reference to the son of the man disappeared from the church's creeds and liturgies like a stone in a lake.

It appears that the public was not ready for the HumanBeing that Jesus knew and called others to relate to. Soon after his death, these aspects fell again into the unconscious and were projected onto the divine Christ. But the apocalypticization of the gospel served an important purpose, nevertheless. It held the urgency of the HumanBeing's "coming," as it were, in suspension, preserving the potential of the HumanBeing for future generations. The apocalyptic gospel has permanently preserved the unconscious contents of the psyche in "constellated" form, ready at any time to irrupt into consciousness. Consequently, all through the history of the church we see new outbreaks of creative energy and vision, as the virtual possibilities are made concrete and actual by fresh seers and prophets. But when the archetypal contents are allowed to remain unconscious, violent explosions of chiliastic zeal follow: crusades, pogroms, inquisitions, holy wars, persecutions, anti-Semitism, and UFO sightings.

I do not wish to leave the impression that the apocalyptic "son of the man" sayings are valueless. I believe that Jesus did look for the final triumph of God in history, that he did await an actual realm of justice and peace, that he felt the urgency of this new reality pressing into the world all the time, and that he lived "as if" that new order was already beginning to dawn. And we can also see that the followers of Jesus were learning to incarnate the "possible human." Solidarity and even identity between Jesus and his disciples began during his ministry, as the Q saying in Matt 10:40 suggests ("Whoever welcomes you welcomes me, and whoever welcomes me welcomes the one who sent me"; parallel Luke 10:16).

As T. W. Manson put it, the disciples can represent Jesus in the fullest sense because they together with him are a *corpus*, the son of the man, the embodiment of the remnant idea in Israel, the organ of God's redemptive purpose in the world.[14] When the early church regarded the ascended HumanBeing as encompassing true humanness, which included Jesus and all others in whom the HumanBeing was alive, they were simply continuing on a new level the partnership they had as *shaliachim*, those sent out in the name of their master.

Thus Jesus' followers did not just speak *in the name of* the HumanBeing, but *as* the HumanBeing. They could speak with the full authority of the HumanBeing because they *were* the HumanBeing speaking. They could heal and cast out demons, not because they had been authorized to do so by the HumanBeing, but because they *were* the HumanBeing healing and exorcising. They could declare sins forgiven without the necessity of sacrifice and temple, not because they had been commissioned to do so by the HumanBeing, but because they *were* the HumanBeing forgiving. Like Jesus, they too had no place to lay their heads; as such they were living the unsettled life of the HumanBeing. Like Jesus, they had early on discovered their own sovereign freedom to decide what is right (Luke 12:57); as such, they were exercising the divine authority of the HumanBeing. Paul said as much when he spoke of the solidarity of redeemed humanity in Jesus as the Second Adam (Rom 5:12–21).

A number of scholars argue that Jesus did not identify with the coming son of the man. For my part, I see the situation as a bit more complicated. Just as he did with the messianic hope, Jesus could neither identify himself without remainder with the son of the man, nor deny that he was living out the son of man in history. So at times he could speak of the HumanBeing as indistinguishable from himself (Matt 11:19//Luke 7:34), and at other times treat it as a corporate entity in which not only he but the disciples (Mark 2:23–28 parallels) and even outsiders could participate (Mark 9:38–41//Luke 9:49–50). The HumanBeing is more than simply Jesus; it represents the future of all humanity, indeed, the whole world, in the purposes of God (Rom 8:18–25). Thus during his active ministry on earth, Jesus could virtually identify with the HumanBeing (while including his disciples occasionally as well), because it was he who was incarnating it and constellating it as an image of transformation. Jesus became the HumanBeing without remainder, but the HumanBeing remained more than Jesus. Logically, A = B, but B is greater than A, with A being Jesus and B the HumanBeing. After his death, resurrection and ascension (and I regard the ascension as a psychic fact on the imaginal plane, not an historical event of the everyday world), the HumanBeing "seated at the right hand of the power of God" became universal. As an archetypal image, as we noted earlier, the HumanBeing now mediates the possibility of becoming more fully human in the image and likeness of God, the Truly Human One. The HumanBeing is a catalytic agent for transformation, providing the form and lure and hunger to become who we were meant to be, or more properly perhaps, to become who we truly are.

These, then, are the questions that have animated my own quest for the historical Jesus:

- Before he was worshiped as God incarnate, how did Jesus struggle to incarnate God?
- Before he became identified as the source of all healing, how did he relate to, and how did he teach his disciples to relate to, the healing Source?
- Before forgiveness became a function solely of his cross, how did Jesus understand people to have been forgiven?
- Before the Kingdom of God became a compensatory afterlife or a future utopia, what did Jesus mean by the Kingdom?
- Before he became identified as Messiah/Christ, how did he relate to the profound meaning in the messianic hope?

Why then did the expression "the son of the man" go so quickly into eclipse? We can now attempt an answer. The early church as reflected in the community that produced Q saw its task as teaching what Jesus taught about the HumanBeing. Thus they continued the ministry of Jesus, perpetuating in their own teaching and healing and exorcism the same sovereign authority that Jesus had exercised and had extended to his disciples during his earthly ministry. Without ever completely abandoning that task, the church increasingly regarded Jesus' cross and resurrection as central. Now the focus was not on carrying forward Jesus' critique of domination, his healing and exorcism, his liberative acts on behalf of those crushed by the domination system. Rather, the focus became the worship of Jesus as the sole divine bearer of salvation.

As H. E. Tödt recognized, a community which calls on the risen Christ and knows that it is addressed by him needs a title which is suitable for calling upon him in worship. The name "the son of the man" cannot be applied in that way. In a Greek speaking context it was semantically grotesque, as has no doubt been drummed into your ears by my insistence on a literal translation of that inelegant phrase. And there is no evidence that the "son of the man" was ever prayed to or made an object of worship in the early church. However, the name *Kyrios*, or Lord, was one that might be invoked in worship. Kyrios was already well known from the Greek version of the Hebrew Scriptures (the Septuagint) and from pagan religions. It was ready made to expand into the new space being created by the church's growing christology. And so the name Jesus had given himself, though preserved in the tradition, was edged out of the church's worship and piety. Thus it virtually disappears, being almost completely absent from the rest of the New Testament, the church's creeds, its doctrines, its liturgies, its devotions, and its reflections on the meaning of Jesus' saving act.[15]

In addition, a burgeoning church hierarchy found the sovereign freedom of the HumanBeing, shall we say . . . inconvenient — as did the Roman Empire once it had nosed into church affairs.

Some of us have become convinced that we not only do not need any longer to worship Jesus, but that we need to *not* worship him. As Rev 22:9 laconically asserts, "Worship God." What we sense as the imperative of the gospel today is to continue Jesus' mission, to unmask the domination system and to liberate those being crushed by it, to open people's lives to the living presence of God, and to foster the process of individuation as we seek to become the people we were made to be. In that process, Jesus will continue to be the human representation of the HumanBeing, without being identified with it. The child of the Human One incarnated by Ezekiel, seen to be entering Godhead in Daniel, and lived into human flesh by Jesus, continues to beckon us in the form of the human Jesus, who had the courage to shoulder a unique revelation of the Mystery into concrete life.

The implications of these reflections are profound. We are freed to go on the journey that Jesus charted rather than to worship the journey of Jesus. We can rescue Jesus from the cloying baggage of christological beliefs unnecessarily added by the church. We are enabled to strip away the heavy accretion of dogma that installed Jesus as the second person of the trinity. Now he can be as available to Jews or Muslims as to Christians, indeed, available to anyone seeking (like Gandhi, for example) to realize the HumanBeing within. We can take Jesus out of the ghetto of the churches and offer him to anyone looking for a guide to true humanity. He was not God in a mansuit, his every step predetermined from all eternity, but a human being seeking the will of God in the everyday decisions that shape life, living, as the Temptation Narrative puts it, by every word that comes from the mouth of God (Matt. 4:4).

Most important, perhaps, Jesus becomes uniquely a criterion of humanness. He shows us something of what it means to become human, but not enough to keep us from having to discover our true humanity ourselves. That means finding in ourselves the same powers that were manifest in Jesus, rather than projecting those powers solely onto him. That means we are to be co-creators with God. It means that we can, if we have the courage, recover the healing ministry of Jesus, and his very Jewish kind of persistent, nagging prayer.

Once again, however, we must warn against turning the numinosity of this real experience of the Human One into a mere idea. God *is* "in the likeness, as it were, of a human being." But God is so much more: nonhuman, subhuman, transhuman, wrapped in thick darkness, incomprehensible, incalculable, unfathomable — yet capable of being experienced, at least fractionally, by everyone. We are all "chips off the old Block," which is to say, we are children of the Human yet mysterious One, and therefore made for communion with our Maker.

And so, dear Fellows and friends, for those of you who wish to build a christology from below, in which the humanity of Jesus is paramount, I offer these reflections on the son of the man. I know no other way we can replace a divinized Christ than through "the son of the man," the HumanBeing. That is why I am convinced that the stone that the builders rejected will indeed become the head of the corner.

Notes

1. Joachim Jeremias thought that in cases where one version of a saying had "I" and the other "the son of the man," that the simple "I" was to be preferred to the solemn son of man expression (*New Testament Theology*, pp. 259–60). But an analysis of each case shows that the earliest form is sometimes the one and sometimes the other. In Matt 5:11, "my" is secondary and the son of the man is primary in the Lukan parallel, 6:22. In Luke's version, Jesus does not identify himself without remainder with the son of

the man, whereas Matthew does so identify him, consistent with his tendency to elevate the christology of his sources. Son of the man is also primary in Luke 12:10 (where Mark 3:28 changes son of the man in Q to "sons of men" to avoid saying that it is all right to blaspheme the son of the man), and in Luke 12:8 (for the same reasons as in Luke 6:22). On the other hand, "I" seems to be the earlier tradition in Luke 22:29 (compare the son of the man in Matt. 19:28). It seems impossible to decide whether Mark 10:45 (with "the son of the man") and Luke 22:27 (without) is the more authentic.

Matthew also adds a number of son of the man references (10:23; 13:37, 41; 16:28; [18:11]; 24:30; 25:31; 26:2). Luke adds [9:56]; 17:22; 18:8; 19:10; 21:36; 22:48; and 24:7.

2. *Ho huios tou anthropou* with the definite article is an almost exclusively Christian term. It is virtually unknown outside the New Testament until the Similitudes of Enoch (and even then, most frequently "*that* son of man"). In postcanonical Hebrew there is only one instance of "*the* son of man," found at Qumran (1QS 11:20), and there the *h* is an addition, written by a scribe over the line. "Thus, with almost complete consistency, the New Testament, whenever the phrase is related to Jesus, adheres to a form which is otherwise virtually unexampled" (C. F. D. Moule, *Essays in New Testament Interpretation*, p. 82).

3. John 12:34 (twice); Luke 24:7; but in each case others are simply quoting Jesus, so these are not genuine exceptions at all.

4. The nine rabbinical instances cited by Geza Vermes are scattered among thousands of pages of Talmudic and other Jewish texts, dated half a millennium later than the gospels ("Appendix E: The Use of *bar nash/bar nasha* in Jewish Aramaic," in Matthew Black, *An Aramaic Approach to the Gospels and Acts*). Only one of the rabbis cited uses the expression twice. Vermes cites eleven texts, but two of them are merely variants of the same story.

5. Douglas R. A. Hare, *The Son of Man Tradition*, p. 23.

6. Morna Hooker, "Is the Son of Man Problem Really Insoluble?" p. 157.

7. Vermes; Maurice Casey, *Son of Man*; Barnabas Lindars, *Jesus Son of Man*; and, omitting the mistranslation theory, Hare.

8. Hare notes that the "messianic secret" in Mark is kept from the public until the end of the story, yet Jesus is represented as referring to himself publicly as "the son of the man" early in the story (2:10, 28). This suggests that the expression "the son of the man" is not understood by Mark as a messianic title (*The Son of Man Tradition*, pp. 181–82).

9. Gerd Theissen, *Biblical Faith*, p. 122.

10. An asterisk (*) indicates author's translation.

11. The discussion is handily summarized by Frederick Houk Borsch, *The Son of Man in Myth and History*.

12. Elizabeth Boyden Howes, *Intersection and Beyond* and *Jesus' Answer to God*.

13. Howes, "Son of Man — Expression of the Self," p. 174.

14. T. W. Manson, *The Teaching of Jesus*, pp. 227, 231.

15. H. E. Tödt, *The Son of Man in the Synoptic Tradition*, pp. 289–90.

Works Consulted

Borsch, Frederick Houk, *The Son of Man in Myth and History*. Philadelphia: Westminster Press, 1967.

Casey, Maurice, *Son of Man*. London: SPCK, 1979.

Jeremias, Joachim, *New Testament Theology*. New York: Charles Scribner's Sons, 1971.

Hare, Douglas R. A., *The Son of Man Tradition*. Minneapolis: Fortress Press, 1990.

Hooker, Morna, "Is the Son of Man Problem Really Insoluble?" In *Text and Interpretation: Studies in the New Testament Presented to Matthew Black*. Ed. Ernest Best and R. McL. Wilson. Cambridge: Cambridge University Press, 1979.

Howes, Elizabeth Boyden, *Intersection and Beyond*. San Francisco: Guild for Psychological Studies, 1971.

____, *Jesus' Answer to God*. San Francisco: Guild for Psychological Studies, 1984.

____, "Son of Man — Expression of the Self."

Lindars, Barnabas, *Jesus Son of Man*. London: SPCK, 1983.

Manson, T. W., *The Teaching of Jesus*. Cambridge: Cambridge University Press, 1959.

Moule, A. D. F., *Essays in New Testament Interpretation*. Cambridge: Cambridge University Press, 1982.

Theissen, Gerd, *Biblical Faith*. Philadelphia: Fortress Press, 1985.

Tödt, H. E., *The Son of Man in the Synoptic Tradition*. Philadelphia: Westminster Press, 1965.

Vermes, Geza, "Appendix E: The Use of bar nash/bar nasha in Jewish Aramaic," in Black, Matthew, *An Aramaic Approach to the Gospels and Acts*. 3rd ed. Oxford: Clarendon Press, 1967.

Contributors

Marcus J. Borg is Hundere Distinguished Professor of Religion and Culture at Oregon State University. He lectures widely throughout North America and abroad, and his books have been translated into German, Dutch, Korean, Japanese, and French. His best-selling works include *The Meaning of Jesus: Two Visions* (with N.T. Wright), *Meeting Jesus Again for the First Time,* and *The God We Never Knew.* He has served as chair of the Historical Jesus Section of the Society of Biblical Literature and co-chair of its International New Testament Program Committee.

John Dominic Crossan is Professor Emeritus of Religious Studies at DePaul University in Chicago. In the past twenty-five years he has written over a dozen books on the historical Jesus, three of which have become religion best sellers: *The Historical Jesus, Jesus: A Revolutionary Biography* and *Who Killed Jesus.* His most recent work is *The Birth of Christianity: Discovering What Happened in the Years Immediately After the Execution of Jesus.* A former co-chair of the Jesus Seminar, he is currently chair of the Historical Jesus Section of the Society of Biblical Literature.

Robert W. Funk is Director of the Westar Institute and founder of the Jesus Seminar. He is a distinguished teacher, writer, translator, and publisher, and is a recognized pioneer in modern biblical scholarship. A Guggenheim Fellow and Senior Fulbright Scholar, he has served as chair of the Graduate Department of Religion at Vanderbilt University and led the Society of Biblical Literature as its Executive Secretary from 1968–1973. His many books include *The Gospel of Jesus, According to the Jesus Seminar, The Five Gospels: The Search for the Authentic Words of Jesus, The Acts of Jesus: The Search for the Authentic Deeds* (all with the Jesus Seminar), and *Honest to Jesus: Jesus for a New Millennium.*

181

Lloyd Geering is Emeritus Professor of Religious Studies at Victoria University of Wellington, New Zealand. Honored as a Companion of the British Empire in 1988, he is a scholar, writer, ordained minister, and renowned and respected commentator on religion. His writings on "The Resurrection of Jesus" in 1967 sparked a two-year controversy, culminating in charges against him by the Presbyterian Church of New Zealand — charges ultimately dismissed after a two-day, nationally televised trial. His books include *The World to Come: From Christian Past to Global Future* and *Tomorrow's God.*

Karen Leigh King is Professor of New Testament Studies and the History of Ancient Christianity at Harvard Divinity School. She has received awards from the National Endowment for the Humanities, the Deutsche Akademische Austauschdienst, Harvard Divinity School, and the Irvine Foundation. In addition to scores of articles, her books include *Images of the Feminine in Gnosticism, Women and Goddess Traditions in Antiquity and Today,* and *Revelation of the Unknowable God.*

Gerd Lüdemann is Professor of New Testament at the University of Germany and Director of the Institute of Early Christian Studies. He has also served as Visiting Scholar at Vanderbilt Divinity School in Nashville and as co-chair of the Society of Biblical Literature Seminar on Jewish Christianity. His many books include *Suppressed Prayers: Gnostic Spirituality in Early Christianity, The Great Deception, The Unholy in Holy Scripture: The Dark Side of the Bible,* and *Heretics: The Other Side of Early Christianity.*

Thomas Sheehan is Professor of Religious Studies at Stanford University. His specialties are the philosophy of religion, twentieth-century European philosophy, and classical metaphysics. A Ford Foundation Fellow, his interests include first-century Christianity and early Jewish and Christian apocalyptic. His books include *The First Coming: How the Kingdom of God Became Christianity,* whose publication in 1986 was one of the earliest popular explorations of the renewed quest of the historical Jesus.

John Shelby Spong has recently retired as Episcopal Bishop of Newark, New Jersey. Raised a fundamentalist in North Carolina, he came to believe that insistence on an inerrant, literal view of the Bible obscures truth and destroys faith. In his many books, he has challenged the Church's position on human sexuality, the virgin birth, and the physical nature of Christ's resurrection. Among his best-selling books are *Rescuing the Bible from Fundamentalism, Resurrection: Myth or Reality?,* and most recently *Why Christianity Must Change or Die: A Bishop Speaks to Believers in Exile.*

Walter Wink is Professor of Biblical Interpretation at Auburn Theological Seminary in New York City. He is an internationally-known lecturer and workshop leader whose areas of interest have been the development of a participative style of Bible study, an exploration of the biblical theme of principalities and powers, and Jesus' teachings on nonviolence. He has led nonviolence workshops around the world, including South Africa, where his work led to his deportation. In 1989–1990 he was honored by selection as a Peace Fellow at the United States Institute of Peace in Washington, D.C. His books include *Homosexuality and Christian Faith: Questions of Conscience for the Churches, The Powers That Be,* and *Cracking the Gnostic Code: The Powers in Gnosticism.*

The Jesus Seminar is a project of the Westar Institute, a membership-supported, nonprofit research and educational organization for the promotion of biblical and religious literacy.

Associate membership in Westar Institute is open to all interested individuals. For more information contact:

Westar Institute
P. O. Box 6144
Santa Rosa, CA 95406
(877) 523-3545
Fax: (707) 523-1350
Email: members@westarinstitute.org
www.westarinstitute.org